THE SIEGE OF GLOUCESTER

By the same author

SHORT STORIES
The Wheat from the Chaff
An Uncertainty of Marriages
Funny Business
More Funny Business

GENERAL FICTION
Time of Departure
Serene Retreat
Johnson's Journey
The Lion and the Lambs
North Flight
Lark Ascending
The Cauldrons of the Storm
Arrow in the Air

SCIENCE FICTION
Aftermath 15
The Charon Tapes
Another Eden
Contact
The King of Hell
Celeste

THE SIEGE OF GLOUCESTER

W. D. PEREIRA

Printed and published by Stoate and Bishop
as their contribution to
the City of Gloucester's Quincentenary Year

First published in Great Britain 1983

ISBN 0 901909 13 0

Stoate and Bishop (Printers) Ltd.
St Catherine Street
Gloucester

Printed in Times Roman
Front Cover by Geoff Maynard

CONTENTS

Mayor's Parlour,
Guildhall,
Gloucester.
GL1 1QG

TELEPHONE NO
0452-22232

February, 1983.

In writing to me about this fascinating book, Mr. Pereira referred to the Siege of Gloucester as a 'little-known engagement' of the Civil War. Personally, I don't think that's quite true - as far as Gloucester people are concerned, at least.

Most locals know that Gloucester sided with Parliament, that there was a siege, and that Gloucester won it. Many visitors to our ancient and remarkable City over the years have been taken down the very narrow alley in Westgate Street and shown the beautiful frontage of Colonel Massey's house, from which the siege was conducted.

Some people will tell you that the nursery rhyme 'Humpty Dumpty' originated at that time, although various versions of the story exist. Others relate that a light was kept burning, throughout the engagement, atop the tower of Gloucester Cathedral, to keep the outlying areas aware that the City was still holding out. You may even be shown an alleged musket ball hole at the east end of the fabric of St. Mary de Crypt church.

But that's about as far as most people's knowledge goes. Details of the pivotal importance of the siege to the Parliamentary cause are hazy. The events leading up to the encounter, and of the actual conduct of the battle aren't usually ready to hand.

Mr. Pereira's book puts flesh on these bones. They give you an insight into the way people in Gloucester lived in those feverish days and weeks. This is a considerable achievement, and one which people well beyond the City boundaries will appreciate.

If you are a Gloucester person - native or adoptive - or if you are one of our considerable band of exiles in other parts of Britain or beyond, this book is required reading. Even if you are not, you'll find a great deal to intrigue you within these covers.

On behalf of my fellow citizens of a City which has been of civic importance for two thousand years, I congratulate Mr. Pereira on his scholarship and creativity and his publishers on their initiative and expertise. I wish the enterprise well.

Peter Arnold

Mayor.
(Councillor Peter Arnold.)

PART ONE

THE CLOSING CIRCLE

It was a still autumn night with a hint of frost in the air. A harvest moon hung swollen and golden against a star studded sky. Faint fumes of smouldering stubble drifted across the City of Gloucester.

There were few lights to be seen. Most of the citizens were asleep preparing for the next day's toil. The only illumination came from braziers beside guarded gates and a few houses whose owners lingered by dying fires.

It was the hour that Faith Merrett liked best. Her heavy work was over and the lighter tasks of merely mending clothes allowed her to relax. She sat on a backless bench by a frame table bearing a single candle. The garments were piled in a wicker basket. Needles and threads lay to hand.

Faith was the second wife of Nathan Merrett the furniture maker. The first had died shortly after twin girls — Anne and Jane — were born. Thus Faith was 24 to her husband's 42. Being Alderman's Pury's daughter, she had poise, intelligence and good looks.

Her fair yellow hair was a crowining glory though concealed on most occasions by a Puritan bonnet. Her face was well structured with large grey eyes being the commanding feature. Her tall figure was, like the hair, hidden by Puritan garb — a grey dress with plain white collar, cuffs and apron.

While Faith sat on a bench in the draughty centre of the room, Nathan occupied a comfortable chair by the fire. He had made the chair for himself. It allowed for his long frame and had wide comfortable armrests. The fire was composed of wood ends, left over from the day's work, and the glow bathed his grim, uncompromising face.

Glancing in his direction, Faith saw a husband who was honest to a fault and downright exasperating. Nathan was a man whose religion wound him up like a spring. He only relaxed when working with wood — shaping and carving, fitting and pegging. He lay rather than sat in the chair, a frown on his brow.

"Where will it end?" The question seemed to come from the depths of Nathan Merrett's soul.

Faith continued mending one of the apprentices shirts. She knew by experience that Nathan, like most men, did not expect an answer to such questions. Particularly from a mere woman. So she would wait patiently and his train of thought might be revealed in due course.

"What is going to happen to us?" her husband came up with another question.

Again Faith kept her silence.

'How quiet,' she reflected, 'the city and our house has become. The twins and apprentices have been asleep for hours. There are little or no sounds outside because of the curfew. Even our home has stopped creaking and settled for the night. There, that is done.' She put the shirt to one side and picked up another.

"My heart," Nathan groaned, "is heavy for us all. For my business that is at a standstill. For you, my wife, if the Royalist devils enter this city. Even for my little daughters in their infant innocence."

"They are but four years of age," Faith ventured a remark.

"Everyone thinks of war," her husband continued as if she had not spoken. "The gentry have barricaded their country houses and declared themselves for the King. We in Gloucester, with the clothmen of Stroud and Dursley, are for Parliament. Families are divided, sons fighting their fathers and emnity between brothers. In Europe, such horrors have continued for decades. It now seems we are to be tried by the Lord."

Nathan Merrett stood up suddenly and crossed the room towards a cupboard. In it was kept the household's most precious possession — a large and heavy leatherbound Bible. Taking the book from the cupboard, he brought it to the table and adjusted the candle for his own use.

"I shall open the Good Book," Nathan said, "and pick a passage at random in the faith and knowledge that the Lord will guide me. And I hope," he said, "comfort me."

Faith sighed inwardly. She feared not the Bible so much as what men made of it.

'Such a method,' Faith recalled, 'had not helped poor Mrs Hyde of Eastgate. The passage selected said she should be put away and Mr Hyde did just that.'

Meanwhile Nathan was praying, his strong hands pressed on the leather cover, his face contorted with emotion. Faith abandoned the mending and lowered her head in unison.

"Guide me O Lord," Nathan Merrett intoned, "so that I may guide myself, my affairs, my household and my wife here." Then with one swift movement, he opened the Bible and stabbed his forefinger on a page.

Nathan's eyes widened at his first sight of the passage. He paused for a long time before reading it out aloud, causing Faith to venture a glance towards him. At last, he intoned,

" 'Come my people. Enter into thy chambers and shut thy doors behind thee. For behold the Lord cometh out of his place to punish the inhabitants of this earth for their iniquity. And the earth shall disclose her blood.' "

There followed an awful silence. In the hearth, a seemingly solid piece of glowing timber collapsed to grey dust.

The Closing Circle

Thomas Hobart, nephew and apprentice to Nathan Merrett the furniture maker, had never been so high before. Even the birds were flying below him. Starlings wheeled over the cathedral close, swifts darted through the cloisters and gulls leaned lazily on the wind.

The sight of the gulls drew his eyes along the widening river. The Severn, he had been told, soon became a channel, a sea, the ocean. There was so much to look at beneath the vast dome of sky, Thomas almost forgot why he had climbed the tower of Gloucester cathedral on an autumn morning in the year 1642.

"Listen to me, lad," Under Sheriff George Hill had instructed him. "I want you walking round the top of that tower like a clock. Looking to north, east, south and west in succession. No sitting down mind. No day dreaming. Why, because for the next two hours the safety of our city will be your responsibility."

Two hours. Tom had already been on the tower two minutes and not moved. What if Hill should see his still figure? What if he had missed Royalist soldiers approaching and not raised the alarm? The under sheriff was a hard man.

Thomas began circling the tower along a wooden catwalk built for that purpose. While keeping an eye on the run of the roads, he could not help surveying the Severn Valley.

From the northern lookout point, he faced up river towards Worcester. To the left lay an end-on view of the pale blue Malverns beyond the bright green of Wainlode Hill. To the right Tewkesbury with its Norman abbey nestled beside the junction of Severn and Avon.

Walking clockwise and looking eastwards the Cotswold escarpment swung into view with outcrops of stone sunbright along the ridges. Thomas identified each hill in turn — Cleeve and Leckhampton, Birdlip and Painswick, Harescombe and Haresfield. Beacons had blazed on them, so the stories went, when the Spanish Armada was defeated.

Again Thomas shifted his position. Now the Cotswolds curved south-westwards, narrowing the gap between hill and river. Bristol thirty-five miles away was out of sight but still remained a neighbour and ally for the Parliamentary cause.

Finally came the west side with wide river and water meadows. There was also the perfect rise of May Hill beside the Forest of Dean uplands where coal was mined and iron smelted. Further still, etched across the horizon, were the Black Mountains of Wales.

By the time he had completed six circuits, Thomas Hobart became bored. There was nothing to report, no one seemingly stirring over the great expanse of countryside.

"There's Uncle Nathan's house," Tom ventured a glance towards Westgate Street, "and the window of my attic room."

From the commanding height of the cathedral tower the city buildings, their roof tops and chimney pots, seemed to be jumbled haphazardly together, leaning this way and that. Tom found it hard to follow the four main streets from The Cross — Northgate, Eastgate, Southgate and Westgate.

Suddenly thunder growled as if reminding him why he was there. He noted the gathering clouds while continuing round the catwalk. More and more thunder sounded across the Severn Valley.

"Pray it does not rain," Thomas muttered for he had come on watch wearing only his shirt and breeches. The clinking sounds of iron-studded boots ascending the stone steps put further thoughts of being drenched out of his head. A moment later, Under Sheriff George Hill appeared through the low doorway.

George Hill was a bull of a man with thick blond curls all over his huge head and down his massive neck. His face was pink and jovial, but the blue eyes were set too close together and always watchful. The under sheriff was wearing his usual leather jerkin and trousers thrust into heavy boots.

"Keeping a sharp lookout, Thomas?"

"Yes, sir."

"Seen anything suspicious?"

"No, sir."

"Hm." Hill began a slow circuit of the catwalk which creaked under his great weight. "You should watch the spaces between the woods. Also the skylines."

The under sheriff moved on with Thomas following at his heels, that is until Hill stopped to point.

"See that dip in the hills. The King's men from Oxford often use it for sorties into the West Country. Remember they have friends and followers as near as Cheltenham and Cranham. Lords, ladies and other grand folk who do not like our workaday city. So you must look carefully for movements and colours. Troops on the march. Flags and pennants. Bright top coats and sashes. The glint of arms and armour."

"Yes sir."

"The same applies across the river. Since Sir John Winter purchased the Forest of Dean from the King, those little miners have been itching to get at us. Behind them are the Welsh. More burrowers who can hardly stand straight. They have always been envious of us upright Gloucester men."

Thomas nodded vigorously. He preferred the under sheriff being so talkative. Hill usually grunted and cuffed boys for the smallest of faults.

By then the clouds looked as if black ink had seeped into them. The Severn was pewter coloured and rain curtains were being drawn across the south western horizon. Thunder rumbled every few seconds, nearer and nearer.

"We'll be used to all sorts of storms," George Hill said, "before it is over." He paused before continuing. "You should know lad that this very day a committee of defence has been set up to put our city on a war footing. Four aldermen no less are on it, led by Mr. Pury of course, with councillors and stewards to do their bidding. I have come from the first meeting."

"It sounds important, sir."

"It is important, lad," Hill assured him. "The watch has been doubled and horses kept ready . . ."

"I can ride, sir." Thomas unwisely interrupted, causing Hill to frown. "My father taught me. At Down Hatherley where I used to live."

"Your parents are dead, lad. You were orphaned and you are now apprenticed to your Uncle Nathan Merrett. Therefore you will do as you are told. Where was I? Ah yes, horses kept ready. I'll tell you something else, Thomas."

"Yes, sir."

"One hundred pounds has been raised to purchase four great cannon for the defence of our city. A gun at each gate, eh. Those Royalists will not find easy pickings here."

"No, sir."

George Hill transferred his gaze from the far distance to the slim, dark haired lad standing beside him.

"Well, see you maintain a good watch." The curtains of rain had almost reached the city. "It takes alertness to win."

"Will we win, sir?"

"Certainly we shall, lad. Four and a half thousand stout citizens of Gloucester are sufficient to take on the whole country. If we need any help, there are thirty thousand more at Bristol. We also have the backing of London with their five hundred thousand. Half a million men! What do you say to that?"

"It is no mean matter," Tom said judiciously, "to oppose a King."

"So do your duty, lad." Under Sheriff Hill ducked under the doorway as heavy rain splattered the cathedral tower.

The second half of October proved mild. There were warm sunny days followed by mild cool nights. This combination at that time of the year produced heavy mists particularly round Gloucester with its river systems, marshlands and water meadows. For about two hours every morning, all that people on the surrounding hills could see of the city were the cathedral tower, church steeples and an occasional chimney pot.

Faith was always the first to rise in the Merrett household. She washed and dressed swiftly, then went across the landing to waken Peggy the maid. That was easier said than done for the girl from Twigworth would burrow deeper into the pile of bedclothes.

Laughing, Faith made sure Peggy was conscious before going to look at the twins, Anne and Jane. They were strange little creatures, still asleep in each other's arms, so she did not rouse them. Instead she descended to the kitchen and lit the fire from woodshavings, sticks and pieces of Forest coal left there the previous evening.

Outside, Faith could not even see the shed in which their two cows were stalled. However she knew the way by heart and was greeted by wet noses. Taking down a bucket and stool, Faith started to milk Mary the nearest cow.

She was soon joined by Thomas. He too took a bucket and stool to milk the other cow Martha, saying politely at the same time,

"Good morning, Aunt Faith."

"A misty one, Thomas. More so than usual. We'll break our fast first, before I take the cows down to the water meadows."

"I can take them if you like, Aunt Faith."

"Thank you, but your uncle expects his apprentices in the workshop. You are not on the Down Hatherley farm now."

"I know."

"Besides," Faith changed the subject, "I wish to see my father this morning and can do that on the way back. He worries, like my husband, about the situation. The constant rumours. The gathering forces of the King."

Thomas nodded and continued to milk Martha. The war hardly concerned him. He had no commitments. Yet he could not help feeling excited whenever there was any news. Military messengers kept riding into the city. And there were now the four guns of Gloucester.

"Aunt Faith."

"Yes Thomas."

"Do you think Uncle Nathan will allow us to go and watch the first cannon being test fired this afternoon?"

"That is up to him Thomas, but I do believe so. As you know, he has little work in hand."

Peggy had breakfast ready on the table when Faith and Thomas arrived with the cans of still warm milk. It consisted of bread and cheese with buttermilk to drink. Eventually everyone — Faith and Thomas, Anne and Jane the twins smiling as always at each other, Peggy the maid and four more yawning apprentices — stood waiting round the table.

They were waiting for Nathan Merrett to put in an appearance. When he arrived, the Puritan furniture maker did not seem to notice anyone. Instead he implored the Lord to bless the food and their day, then seated himself without another word. At the end of their meal however Nathan pronounced,

"As we have insufficient work and, provided everyone behaves, we shall go to witness the first cannon being fired this afternoon."

After the meal, Nathan led his apprentices to the workshop leaving Faith and Peggy to get on with their daily tasks. The moment he left, Mrs Curtis a widow woman who helped about the house and looked after the twins put in an apprearance.

"They do say," said Mrs Curtis, who managed to keep abreast of the news and gossip, "that there be strange riders out and about. Not only on the hills, but coming and going about the valley."

"Who are they?" Peggy asked excitedly. Despite a strict Puritan upbringing, the pretty maid had recurrent dreams of being swept off her feet by a handsome cavalier.

"Not many knows," Mrs Curtis implied that she was much better informed, "so the watchmen are taking no chances. There be great chains strung across each gateway and, I should tell you Mistress Merrett, that cattle must graze on the near pastures."

"Thank you for the information," said Faith.

The cows knew their way blindfold. Mary and Martha were also uncommonly placid creatures and never interfered with the Westgate Street stalls or open fronted shops. It was not long before they reached the blocked bridge.

" 'Morning Mrs Merrett!" James Wood, the chief sheriff greeted her. "I am afraid the far meadows are not being used today. Riders have been seen. There is something stirring."

"It makes little difference to Mary and Martha," Faith replied. "See my cows are already on their way to the near pastures."

Faith was turning to leave when the sound of shouting attracted her attention. Everyone else was equally alerted — the sheriff, the watchers by the gate and washerwomen carrying clothes to the river. One and all they looked towards an excited crowd moving from the city towards the water's edge.

The crowd consisted of about a hundred citizens milling round a group of apprentices distinguishable by their close cropped heads. Three of the lads were leading horses, while others wrestled with unseen men in their midst. As Faith watched, she saw Under Sheriff George Hill handing out swords, pistols, armour and pieces of clothing.

"There now!" Hill shouted when the apprentices fell back to reveal three near naked men. "You won't be too weighed down for your swimming."

"I'll remember you," one of the men began, but became silent when the bull-like under sheriff made a move towards him. Hill said,

"You may enter our river the hard way or the easy way. Head first or of your own accord."

"Damn you!" the man cried then led the two others into the water. The crowd watched silently as the three men sank to their waists, chests and necks before striking out for the far shore. They emerged dripping and the first man shouted as he shook his fist,

"I shall not forget you Under Sheriff George Hill!" With that, he and his two companions set off, still dripping and shivering, across the misty countryside.

"Who were they?" Wood asked Hill.

"Royalist recruiting party," the under sheriff sniggered. "Fancy coming to Gloucester of all places. We are now better off by three fine horses and some valuable arms."

"Their leader looked familiar," said the sheriff, "and a gentleman to boot. Do you know who he was?"

"He kept telling me," Hill smirked, "that his name was Sir Ralph Dutton."

"You aim high, George. If Dutton returns with his friends, the city gibbet will not be tall enough for you."

When Faith arrived at the Town Hall, councillors were leaving the chamber. Their faces, she observed, were grave and, although all of them knew her, they merely bowed in passing. Only John Dorney the town clerk came over to greet her.

"I am glad you are here," he said. "Your father's spirits are low."

"Bad news?"

"Unfortunately yes." Dorney held the door open for her.

Alderman Pury was not in the council chamber but had retired to his inner office. He sat at a document covered table, an austere figure in fine yet sombre clothes. His face, grave as those of the councillors, brightened on seeing Faith.

"It is good to see you, my daughter."

"And you, father." She kissed him then sat down. "How is mother?"

"Her aches and pains are no better." Alderman Pury made the stock reply about his bedridden wife. "I have had news from Alan." He was referring to his eldest son and Faith's favourite brother. "He is returning from his military training in Bristol to be a captain in our town regiment."

"I am glad," Faith said and her father nodded.

"That is about all the good news, for our cause is not doing well. At least not in the countryside. Away from London and a few towns, men flock to join the King. They are assembling in the north and the south west, in the Midlands and in Wales. They have been joined by the King's nephews, the Princes Rupert and Maurice, both highly skilled cavalry commanders from Germany. And you know what Germans are like."

This time Faith nodded.

"But you do not know the latest news, because it has not yet been released. Already Rupert's cavalry have routed a strong Parliamentary force at Powick Bridge."

"Where is that, father?"

"Too near for us, Faith. Between Tewkesbury and Worcester. As we speak, King Charles with his main force is leaving Oxford. He has sworn to destroy our patched together army under the Earl of Essex."

"What of here, father?'

"Here we are short of everything, beginning with money. Parliament voted us £1000 but, with Royalists swarming between London and Gloucester, it was considered too great a risk to convey such a sum. So we are left to our own resources and decided to sell the corporation plate."

"Who would buy?"

"The astute who profit in all circumstances. Certain leading citizens have already done so at shamelessly low prices." Pury consulted a document on his desk. "Two gilt bowls, a gilt tankard and a solid silver one, the mayoral seal and four jewelled maces realised £46-4-6d." Faith's father paused before continuing, "This morning it was agreed that councillors should contribute personally before taxing the citizens. To show example. The mayor and alderman are to give 16/8d each. Sheriffs and their equals 13/4d. The rest 10 shillings. There have been some hard arguments, I can tell you." A bleak smile appeared on Alderman Pury's face, the faded. He said

"We would prefer to be left alone, but our enemies are strong and ruthless. I must say this Faith, to prepare you. You may live to see your father dragged on a hurdle along that street to hang from the city gibbet."

"Oh father!" Faith put her arms round him.

"Only to you, my daughter, do I dare speak such faint-hearted words. Enought of them." He gently detached himself. "Are you coming to see the first of our cannon being fired this afternoon?"

"We shall be there, father," she affirmed.

New emplacements were being made for Gloucester's cannon in the crumbling walls. Each gun would be attended by a master gunner and two assistants, all of whom had already cost the city a pretty penny.

The Eastgate emplacement was the first to be completed. Cannon balls had been stacked to one side while on the other were tools of the trade — budge barrels containing gunpowder, iron ladles and ram rods, sponges and wadding, together with mallets, wedges and buckets of water.

Two leather clad assistants stood proudly by the cannon as Master Gunner Hatton addressed the assembly. He was a vain little man with twitching eyebrows, determined to make the most of the occasion.

"My Lord Mayor, Aldermen, Councillors and Citizens of Gloucester, you are looking at the ultimate weapon in the long and fearful history of warfare. This brass cannon," he patted it, "is called a culverin. It weighs 4000 pounds and can fire up to 18 pounds of shot. Firing however may only be achieved by expert knowledge, such as I possess, and following the most meticulous drill, which I shall describe to you."

"Perhaps," said Dennis Wise the mayor, "you could demonstrate as you describe. We have much else to do."

Hatton's eyebrows twitched frantically.

"Of course, sir." The next moment he lifted his head and shouted in a strangely strangled voice, "Put back your piece!"

A ripple of laughter ran through the crowd when one of the assistants pointed out that, because the gun had not yet been fired, it was not in the recoil position. But Hatton was determined to go through the twelve commands of gunnery drill.

"Order your piece!"

This entailed removing the elevating wedge and so raising the muzzle for loading.

"Sponge your piece! That sir," Hatton explained to the mayor, "is to remove smouldering debris from the last firing."

"Very essential," Wise agreed.

"Fill your ladle!" The shrieked command caused one of the assistants to grab a ladle while the other poured black powder from the topmost budge barrel. The crowd grew quiet.

"Empty your ladle!" Hatton shouted and his assistant poured powder down the barrel.

"Ram home your powder!" Hatton screamed to his other assistant. "Thrust home your wad!" He turned to the first who promptly dropped the ladle and picked up wadding to keep the gunpowder in place, "Regard your shot!"

This order entailed taking a cannon ball to inspect it for correct size and any imperfections. The citizens grew restless again until Master Gunner Hatton, his eyebrows in constant agitation, ordered,

"Put home your shot!" The iron ball rolled down the barrel, then Hatton addressed both his assistants, "Thrust home your last!" This entailed inserting and ramming home a second piece of wadding to retain the ball.

"Sir," Hatton addressed the mayor, "your cannon is ready for firing."

"Then fire it, master gunner."

"Gauge your piece!" Hatton shouted for his own benefit, as he now had to sight the gun on a white canvas target across several fields.

Finally the master gunner took a smouldering linstock from his assistant and applied it to the touch hole of the cannon. There followed a tremendous roar which caused everyone to jump back. The gun also bounced backwards and, when the acrid smoke had cleared, the white canvas target was seen to be untouched.

"I was watching the town clock," Nathan Merrett said to Faith on their way home. "It took all of four minutes to miss the mark. By then Prince Rupert's troopers could have stormed the place and had us all hanging from gibbets."

Faith shivered. It was the third time she had heard that ominous word in one day. The twins beside her were smirking as usual. Sometimes she wanted to slap them.

The freezing fogs of early November did not please the watchers at the city gates. Apart from being chilled to the bone, they feared what might come at them out of the murk. Skirmishes were taking place throughout the Severn Valley and there had been a battle, it was rumoured, at somewhere called Edgehill.

Such tales were spread by tobacco farmers from Cheltenham. They told how the King's army had wiped out the Parliamentary forces, though this was taken with a pinch of salt by the Gloucester citizens. Everyone knew that the ridiculous little townlet of Cheltenham had Royalist pretensions.

Fear nevertheless lurked in the thickened air. Every man on guard thought of the dreaded dragoons, with swords drawn, charging in among them. The weather was icy enough without the added hazard of cold steel.

Suddenly the Northgate watch heard the clinking of harness. The alert was given, reinforcements called for and word sent to the committee of defence. By the time a young officer wearing an orange coloured Parliamentary sash loomed out of the fog, there were a score of muskets and pistols pointing at him.

The officer was followed by two weary regiments and many wounded in carts. Word was given to pass them though and the soldiers shuffled along Northgate Street to The Cross. Musketeers alternated with pikemen. Finally the wounded were hauled into the city.

Plans provisionally made for billeting soldiers — at 3 shillings a week per man — were put into effect. Aldermen were required to take six men, councillors five, sheriffs and their equals four, then the rest of the population 'in similar proportion'.

Thus Faith Merrett had three soldiers billeted on her. She did not mind this but Nathan was critical. Fighting men, he declared, should either sleep in barns or the open fields.

"Corporal Cready and me," said a Sergeant Musgrave, propping his halbert by the kitchen door, "would be grateful for any warmth and food you can offer us."

"I can give you both," Faith promised them.

"However," the Sergeant went on, "Lieutenant Gwinnett out there is another matter." He nodded towards a high-sided farm cart.

"What's wrong with him?" Faith took a deep breath.

"Sword cut. Yesterday evening. A Royalist troop attacked us near Evesham. Gwinnett took one across the thigh. It's deep."

"Bring him in and we'll try to help. Peggy, fetch a blanket for the kitchen table. Mrs Curtis, take the twins upstairs. Tom, stoke the fire and set two cauldrons of water on it."

Everyone rushed to do Faith's bidding, secretly relieved that they were not in charge. A minute later the lieutenant lay on the table. He was semi-conscious, his unseeing eyes turned upwards, his skin like dirty wax exuding moisture. While the blood-soaked clothes were being cut away, he made low moaning sounds.

"Dear God!" Peggy came close to blasphemy when she saw the wound. She started to retch.

"Outside!" her mistress sounded cross though in reality Faith welcomed any diversion. For Lieutenant Gwinnett's wound was of butcher shop ghastliness, the bruised flesh laid back to the bone.

"Needs sewing up," Sergeant Musgrave said in a matter of fact voice.

"I can sew," Faith heard herself saying. She shook her head to try and clear it, then issued more orders. "Tom, bring straps from the stables. Also tell Peggy to put my stock of marigold seeds in a pan of water and boil them. Sergeant, I shall be relying on you and your corporal to keep him quiet."

"For that we need a wooden spoon. As a gag."

Faith never knew how she got through the next half hour. Fortunately Thomas managed to help her, even by pressing the wound together for the stitching. At last she was able to apply a compress soaked in the boiled marigold water for congealing and healing the wound.

For three days and nights, Faith nursed the officer, forever bathing his fevered face in cool water. On the fourth morning Gwinnett asked for food and swallowed some broth. After that he made a rapid recovery.

"Fortunately I am a good healer," the lieutenant said to Thomas, "which is necessary in my profession. I find it ironic, coming through the Battle of Edgehill without a scratch, then being wounded in a skirmish."

"Were you at Edgehill?"

"Aye, with Sir Thomas Ballard." Gwinnett replied. "We kept our line all day and, because of our stubborness, the King withdrew his army at nightfall. I would not call it a victory by either side though we were left in possession of the field."

Lieutenant Richard Gwinnett made a rapid recovery and within a fortnight was limping about the place. Even Nathan Merrett grudgingly admired his courage and began discussing military matters with the officer. One evening Nathan came smiling to the supper table.

"News has reached us," he announced, "of the King being turned back outside London. He marched from his Oxford headquarters with Prince

Rupert's horse ahead of him in an attempt to take the capital."

Nathan paused as everyone was hanging on his words.

"Last Saturday," he went on, "Rupert did manage to occupy a village called Brentford but, that evening, the trained bands of Parliament marched out to meet him and his master. For all of Sunday our gallant lads stood shoulder to shoulder facing the King's men at Turnham Green. Charles saw there was no way past them and in the end returned to Oxford."

"Hm." Gwinnett did not appear pleased.

"Are you not glad of our victory, lieutenant?"

"It is no real victory — like Edgehill. With London blocked, the King will turn his attention in other directions. Perhaps towards us."

The darkening days of 1642 were reflected in the thoughts of most Gloucester citizens. Every item of news to reach them was bad. Everywhere the King's cause seemed to be succeeding. The Cotswolds swarmed with Royalists. The Midlands, apart from Warwick and Coventry, declared for the monarch. Cornishmen were gathering to launch a deadly campaign in the West Country. From Wales, forces moved to Coleford.

Within the city, Parliamentary troops came and went. Commanders conferred and regiments marched, including that of Lieutenant Gwinnett. One day soldiers with familiar faces would be guarding Gloucester, the next they were moving to other places deemed to be of greater strategic value.

While he was not working or on duty, Thomas Hobart roamed the city absorbing the sights and soaking up information. He watched volunteers and recruited men being issued with uniforms and arms. The foot soldiers consisted of musketeers and pikemen in the rough proportion of two to one. The horsemen were mostly made up of dragoons who combined mounted mobility with the ability to fight on foot.

Thomas noted that musketeers wore no body armour though, crossing from the shoulders down to their hips, were two wide bands of thick leather. A sword hung on the lower left side and suspended from the other band were the necessities of musketry. These comprised a flask of gunpowder and a priming horn, a leather bag containing spare bullets and a dozen made-up cartridges known as The Twelve Apostles.

Around their necks, musketeers also wore large leather collars to help protect their shoulders from sword cuts, pike thrusts and, when on the march, the chafing of the heavy muskets. On their heads they had wide brimmed felt hats with in many cases, as Thomas learned, steel skull caps underneath them.

As for the pikemen, they were selected for their size and strength. They wore iron helmets, breast and back plates supplemented by gorgets of iron at the neck and articulated tassets down their front thighs. Their pikes were of long, straight ash with 4 foot steel spikes riveted to the 14 foot poles.

Around the city, cavalrymen were being taught to form and wheel, to draw pistols from saddle holsters and fire them so their horses grew accustomed to the sudden shots. In addition to two pistols, many cavalrymen carried a short musket or carbine hung loosely round their necks by leather straps. These were fired then left dangling while the fight continued with drawn swords.

The city fathers however were more concerned with the preservation of Gloucester than the constant drilling and other military activities. Long days and weary nights were spent dealing with myriad matters. No wonder Faith began to worry about her father's health.

"London keeps assuring us of our importance," Alderman Pury addressed the committee of defence, "but how has Parliament served us? We need money that never arrives, so we have to raise it ourselves. We need a strong garrison of soldiers, yet they come and go.

"Some at least remain," said Dennis Wise the mayor, "and we are here to appoint a military governor. There are two schools of thought on the matter. One is that we should have a local man, known and loyal to us. The other is to put our fate in the hands of a professional soldier.

"For my part," Councillor Nicholas Webb leaned forward, "I favour a local man." His hand held a sheet of paper. "I have here three names of leading citizens with military experience. If we can agree in principle to have a Gloucester man, then we could quickly proceed to the actual selection."

"I would second that," said Sheriff James Wood. "We trust one another because we know one another. We live here and Gloucester is our home. Can we put our trust in an officer who has left his home? It is no matter to such a person where he fights, who he defends. These professional soldiers, I note, know more of each other — on both sides. It is a game to them though not to us."

"Surely," said Alderman Pury, "it is no game to risk one's life. I believe in using specialists, therefore a military man for military matters. I say we put it to the vote."

They voted and the majority opted for a professional soldier.

"I am glad," Alderman Pury commented, "we have not flouted the wishes of Parliament — namely, that we appoint Lieutenant Colonel Edward Massey. He is here and he is already active in our cause. The appointment would rest well on his shoulders."

"Massey is an unknown quantity," Webb continued to object. "No one knows much about him. Some say he was an apprentice on London Bridge before running away . . ."

"To become a soldier in the Low Countries," Mayor Wise pointed out.

"He ran away all the same. Not a good example to our own apprentices. Let us also not forget Massey returned to England but three years ago and served in the King's army. Only when Massey was dissatisfied with his lack of preferment, did he change sides."

"I find him an awkward man," Councillor Tobias Jordan, the city's leading Puritan remarked.

"Give me awkward men," Pury insisted, "rather than the complacent. They may be likened to the piece of grit in an oyster which produces the pearl. I appreciate that Massey has been with us but a short while, yet see how hard he works, how active he is on our behalf. Are we to reject him for that? I put it to a second vote."

There was a clear majority for Colonel Massey's appointment, though Councillors Webb and Jordan still objected.

"I think we have made the wrong decision," was Webb's comment and Jordan added,

"Massey still has to prove himself to me."

"Then you, Tobias," Aldermen Pury said "can act as liaison between this committee and the military."

There was no public acclaim on Massey's appointment. Like Tobias Jordan, Gloucester citizens had a traditional wait-and-see attitude to people and events. They were slow to act, while the slightly built 23-year old colonel seemed intent on disrupting their lives. For Massey was everywhere at all hours — constantly moving about the city, drilling men and recruiting others. This was how Thomas Hobart came to the colonel's notice.

Among the many notices put up at The Cross was one to the effect that gallopers were needed. A galloper had to be young, light and able to ride well. Such riders, Massey wrote, were to become the eyes of his force, scouring the surrounding countryside for information. Later he stood watching one young man after another select the best chargers then race up and down Gaudy Green.

"I suppose you want a charger too?" he said to Thomas who was next in the line.

"No, sir," the lad replied, "I'll settle for that yellow pony".

"Would you now?" Massey followed his gaze.

Tom went and spoke to the pony before slipping a bridle over its head. He had learned from his father that it was not so much what one said but the tone of voice used. Thus he captured and held the pony's attention. Several of Massey's men began to fret at the delay but their normally impatient colonel remained impassive.

Then Thomas was up on the pony's bare back. He made the creature trot and canter before galloping. He also lay low on its back and moved as far as possible to each side without stirrups. Finally Tom jumped off and on at the gallop.

"You shall be my galloper," Colonel Massey said on his return.

"Thank you, sir."

"What is your name?"

"Thomas Hobart, sir."

"An apprentice?"

"To Nathan Merrett, furniture maker of Westgate Street."

"He'll not be making much furniture in these troubled times, so tell him, Tom, I have need of you."

Edward Massey's dark eyes never left the lad's face as he was talking. For his part, Thomas saw a stern countenance, made sterner by the upcurled military moustache and small beard of the day. The colonel's hair was black and long, framing a sallow, slightly pock-marked complexion.

"Sergeant Major Pudsey," Massey turned to a big powerfully built man beside him, "Thomas Hobart goes on our strength."

Early each morning Thomas reported to Massey and was sent to help in the horse lines. Later, when the colonel made the old dilapidated Greyfriars Priory his headquarters, Tom slept and ate there — again with the horses.

One ray of hope flickered during the dark December days. News came through that Parliamentary forces under Sir William Waller — a Devonshire man and a friend of Massey — had taken Winchester from the King.

There were no more glad tidings of this nature and winter gloom descended again. Christmas in Puritan Gloucester was a subdued affair. Soldiers who attempted to celebrate in the city taverns were firmly discouraged. Even the traditional midnight gathering at The Cross to welcome the New Year was muted. A hard core of revellers went there, lost heart and trailed home.

"Tonight has been like any other night," John Dorney the town clerk wrote in his diary, "but what 1643 will bring to Gloucester is another matter."

On New Year's Day, Lieutenant Colonel Edward Massey called a conference of his captains. They consisted of Captains Bassett, Blunt, Crispe, Faulkner, Gray, Harcus, Mallery, Moore and Alan Pury, Faith's brother who had returned from his Bristol training for duty at Gloucester.

Included at the meeting were Sergeant Major Henry Pudsey and Councillor Tobias Jordan.

The officers made a brave showing with their burnished body armour, intricately wrought swords and bright orange sashes. Their leather boots, gauntlets, buff coats, belts and straps creaked as they moved. Only Jordan, wearing dark Puritan clothes, looked sombre.

"Gentlemen," Massey began briskly, "being all gathered together on this first day of the year leads me to wonder how many of us will be here for the last. I suspect that some of our number will be missing — including perhaps myself. For the forces against us are formidable and our only chance of winning fraught with danger. I say to you now, if any man feels unwilling to share the dangers, he should forthwith depart from our company."

"Leaving us," Pudsey added, "his arms and armour."

No one moved.

"Our main task is threefold," their colonel continued. "First and foremost we have to hold this city, sited at the crossroads of England, for Parliament." Massey turned to Jordan. "It will mean much more work on the fortifications, councillor. They are quite inadequate and I speak as one trained in siege engineering. I have been round the walls — or what is left of them — and shall do so again this morning with Sergeant Major Pudsey. He will make a list of my requirements for your committee's consideration."

"It is all a matter of money . . ." Jordan started to say.

"And survival," Massey stressed. "The second part, gentlemen, entails maintaining outpost garrisons. As you know, these help keep the way open to other Parliamentary towns — Bristol to the south west, Warwick and Coventry in the Midlands. Some garrisons are small and scattered at such places as Cirencester and Stroud, Dursley and Berkeley. We shall have difficulty holding them. Therefore we should maintain them for as long as we can while remembering that Gloucester is our chief concern."

"Quite so," Tobias Jordan agreed.

"In total we have 1500 soldiers, most of whom are at present strung across the countryside, and we are training some 500 citizens. We cannot afford to waste them, gentlemen. If any outpost becomes untenable, you have my approval to make a local decision. It is 'Pull out and fall back on Gloucester.' "

"The committee of defence," said Jordan, "will be pleased to hear of your ruling, colonel."

"Which must not be made public, sir," Massey retorted. "The third part is that of communications. A commander has to rely on information in order to make decisions. The right information for the right decisions. I lay great stress on this. It is the reason why I have arranged for such a large proportion of gallopers. Six per troop. Four others standing by at each city gate. My own band of riders."

Massey paused then concluded,

"Well, that is it, gentlemen. You have been told of my general plans. You will be receiving more specific orders in the days that lie ahead. Let us hope and pray the New Year will prove satisfactory to our cause."

After the meeting had broken up, Pudsey asked,

"What now, Edward?"

"Let us go on one of my prowls." Massey gave an unexpected smile. "Yes Henry, I am well aware that Jordan tells his committee how I am always prowling around the city. There is however no other way to get the feel of a place."

"Agreed. By horse or on foot?"

"Horses," the colonel said briskly. "To begin with."

Outside, the light snowfall of the night was being supplemented by drifting flakes. Heavy yellow clouds indicated more snow to come. The horses moved warily on the slippery ground, rolling their eyes at each other and exchanging puffs of vapour.

From his Greyfriars headquarters, Massey made for the main guardroom close to The Cross. This was sited in the Wheat Market and housed 120 men. Next he visited the church of St Mary de Crypt, where ammunition was stored, also a nearby mill set up to make gunpowder.

"How is production going?" Massey asked Pudsey.

"We are up to one and a half budge barrels a week."

"Still far too low."

"It is both difficult and dangerous, Edward. You know that."

"Then establish a second mill in case the first destroys itself."

Massey now headed for Westgate Bridge. On his approach, the watch sprang to attention and hastened to remove the chain when their colonel stated that he wished to cross the river. As Massey rode on and on, Pudsey began to wonder where they were going. At last they halted.

"The old Bishop's Palace." Massey gazed towards the once splendid building on the island of Over. "There must be plenty of lead left on those massive rooves, Henry. Rip it out. We shall be needing all the bullets we can make."

"With due respect," Pudsey became formal, "Gloucester still contains many followers of the Established Church. Vandalism of that particular building might upset them."

"So do not seem to upset them. Quietly bring a squad here each morning and they can spend the afternoons making bullets. It will also be a precedent in case we have to occupy and fortify the place."

Edward Massey turned his horse's head and they rode back to the bridge. Once across the river, the two officers continued their tour of inspection. From Westgate round to Northgate there were no walls. Instead, earthworks ran beside the snow-mantled marshes.

"It is unlikely," the colonel commented, "that any major attack will be made against this quarter. Nevertheless Henry, those earthworks need to be half as high again. Inform Councillor Jordan. If he wants us to defend his city, its citizens must help more."

Though somewhat higher earthworks extended from Northgate to Eastgate, the city wall proper only commenced at a postern near to the latter entrance. This arrangement, Colonel Massey declared, constituted a weak spot.

"And has to be strengthened. Considerably. Here the earthworks must be twice as high and a deep ditch is required on the outer side. We also need at least six cannon for the defence of the sector."

"Six?"

"Yes, I know the difficulties you are encountering in trying to buy another four guns. Well I shall be wanting a score or more before I am finished. Those that cannot be bought will have to be captured."

They rode on through a sudden swirl of snow. Beyond Eastgate, the old city wall rose above them. It looked solid enough, but Massey was still not satisfied. He voiced his thoughts as they progressed,

"Too flimsy to withstand modern artillery. Insufficient foundations for the guns you are going to get. Far too many houses outside the walls. Their inhabitants must come into the city and their homes put to the torch. We are in a brutish business, Henry, a brutish business."

The final sector from Southgate back to Westgate worried Colonel Massey most of all. Heavy snow began to obliterate the scene as he made his way between the castle and the docks, but both men knew it well.

"You will need," Massey said, "to concentrate cannon here, along the Bristol Road. If it comes to a siege, I warrant we shall see the main action in this sector. On Gaudy Green and in the grounds of Llanthony Priory."

They reached the river again and picked their way between warehouses to the Butter Market.

"Food!" the Governor exclaimed. "Something else to think about, Henry. Or rather, get the city fathers thinking on it. The mathematics are 4500 citizens, 1500 soldiers and upwards of 1000 refugees multiplied by three meals a day."

"John Dorney has plans."

"Good, but make sure they are put into effect. I shall do a little more prowling," Colonel Massey said when they reached Greyfriars and troopers led away their horses. "On foot. Sometimes one learns a great deal that way."

Massey was off again, his usually sharp footsteps now silenced by a carpet of snow. The colonel liked to try and obtain what he called 'a sense of place'.

As a starting point, he went to the city centre. The Cross was a tall stone building originally erected by the Old Religion. Royalist proclamations had once been read there though of late these were replaced by Parliamentary and civic manifestos.

Each of the city's four main streets, Edward Massey had previously noted, possessed a character of its own. Starting with Northgate, this contained the ancient inappropriately named New Inn, also the Cordwainery. The latter comprised a group of shops and stalls where leathergoods — such as boots and shoes, coats and belts, saddles and bridles — were made and sold. Cordwainery traders, Massey had discovered, were the same in every town and country. Laughing and joking, he went among them and hinted of more business to come.

Next, retracing his steps past the New Inn, Massey went by The Cross into Southgate Street. In contrast to busy Northgate, this was a quiet thoroughfare. At one time it had been a street of churches. These were still standing, but now most served as warehouses and even stables. The least ornate were used by Puritans who sat doggedly with their hats on during three hour sermons.

Finding no one to talk to, Edward Massey cut through alleyways to Eastgate, the business and commercial centre of Gloucester. Once the street was favoured by rich men keeping kings on thrones through loans of money. These days, the Colonel reflected, merchants tend to do the opposite. Nevertheless he smiled and bowed at everyone.

Finally Massey walked down Westgate, Gloucester's longest street which ran all the way to the Severn. Even on that snowy morning the open-fronted shops and stalls were doing business. Again the colonel made a point of speaking to as many people as possible.

Further down Westgate Street were the butchers of Gloucester with their sturdy work tables round a central slaughter house. Further still came the goldsmiths and silversmiths, trades that continued to flourish at all times. Beyond them were the makers of pewterware, coppersmiths and ironsmiths. Formerly, most of the smiths had worked on farm implements, but now they laboured with helmets and body armour. Furnaces roared, hammers rose and fell, swords shrieked on cutlers' grindstones.

Edward Massey was in his element talking to the smiths and cutlers.

"These heavy swords coming from Germany," said one man. "I should not like to be hit with one."

"Nor I," Massey agreed, taking the sword in his hand. It was an awesome weapon, the steel blade perfectly balanced by the iron guard and handle. "In the Low Countries they have become known as 'mortuary swords'. It will be the same here."

"Such elaborate chiselling on the guard," said another man. "Basketwork. Foreign faces. Caballistic insignia. What does 1414 mean, Colonel?"

"From the Book of Job," Massey answered. "Chapter 14, Verse 14. 'If a man die, shall he live again?'"

A hush came over the small gathering. It was a weighty question.

As he moved away from the furnaces, Colonel Massey suddenly felt cold. The streets were cheerless in contrast with the fine snug houses of the rich. He paused to gaze up at Alderman Pury's mansion and, at that moment, peels of laughter came from an upstairs window.

Such merriment from the house of the city's leading Puritan caused Massey to frown. He lingered and heard it again, though not so loud this time. 'Servants perhaps,' the colonel reflected before continuing his way to Greyfriars headquarters and a bowl of stew.

The laughter had come from Mrs Hortense Pury, the bedridden and usually complaining wife of the Alderman. She occupied the first floor bedroom which was the biggest and best in the house. A fire burned there winter and summer and the room had become Mrs Pury's whole world. Usually she fretted and sulked. Only when Alan and Faith visited her was she happy.

" 'The third part is that of communications,' " Young Captain Pury quoted from Colonel Massey, at the same time brandishing a drawn sword. " 'A commander has to rely on information in order to make decisions. The right information for the right decisions.' "

"He didn't," his mother giggled, "he didn't say that?" She had once been beautiful, but fat and discontent had taken their toll. "It is as good as a bad play."

"A play, mother," Alan teased her. "Tut, tut."

"Ah yes," she became serious. "What would your father say? But I did like plays." Tears of self pity welled up in her eyes. "And dancing. Did I ever tell you about when we lived in London? When your father was a member of parliament?"

'You tell us every time, mother,' Faith reflected yet smiled encouragingly.

"It was so nice," Hortense Pury recollected. "We had our own house in London and your father was well regarded both by King and Parliament. We were invited to the court — I wore a pale saffron coloured dress — and King Charles was so nice to me. So was Queen Henrietta."

"We were also friends of the Pyms. John Pym, such a nice man. I may be a stupid woman, but I could never see why the King and John did not have a quiet talk, then come to some reasonable agreement. Anything would be better than the circumstances in which we now find ourselves with the King's soldiers nearly at our gates."

"Not quite at our gates, mother." Alan gave her a playful squeeze. "There are a few stout soldiers on our side, including your own son."

"So unnecessary," Mrs Pury fretted. "So unnecessary."

"I am inclined to agree," Faith rose and smoothed her dress. "It is time for me to leave and see about some food for my household, though only the Lord knows where the money to purchase it is coming from. Nathan hardly has any work these days and he will not borrow. He even resents soldiers being billeted on us. Let us hope and pray that the war soon passes us by."

Suddenly war came to Gloucester. It arrived on a wet February morning in the form of a wild-eyed rider on a foam-flecked horse. He was from Cirencester which had been stormed and taken by Prince Rupert's cavalry. The man babbled his tale to the guards at Eastgate and, within minutes, the dreaded news was round the city.

Colonel Massey immediately ordered a full alert. All that day, soldiers lined the walls and citizens the earthworks. Those living outside came to shelter within the city. Scouts and gallopers probed south eastwards for any sign of the Prince from Germany.

Twenty-four hours passed in this way. Thomas spent the night at Greyfriars headquarters helping to look after the horses. He was asleep when a rough hand shook him. It was the colonel's groom.

"They're coming. We have to assemble the horses behind Eastgate."

Thus Thomas found himself leading two chargers who seemed to have caught the scent of coming battle. It was all he could do to avoid their dancing hooves. Tom was glad to hand them over to their owners who immediately checked every strap. Men everywhere were priming muskets and pistols.

As yet, Tom was still below the wall. He wondered if anyone would object to him mounting the steps for a better view. The soldiers seemed too busy to notice. Besides he was one of Colonel Massey's chosen gallopers. Where better than close to his master's side?

Even on the battlements, no one glanced at him — but then they had so much else to see. Following their gaze, Tom discerned a column of cavalry growing as it were out of Hucclecote Woods. The horsemen rode three abreast and, at their head, an ensign carried the colours.

"A full regiment would you say?" Massey asked Pudsey.

"More than full."

"Aye, princes need no recruiting officers. Fortunately, not even Prince Rupert can take us with a single regiment. I warrant he will try to bluff. 'In the name of the King." Massey gave a mirthless smile.

For the next half hour, the Royalists made their way towards Gloucester. They did not hurry though, as Thomas noted, they moved with purpose. Most were big men mounted on large warhorses. Their armour was elaborate, their swords heavy.

"Germans many of them." remarked a corporal standing next to Thomas. "Rhinelanders. Cut you to pieces as soon as look at you."

"Where's Prince Rupert?"

"He will be with that troop moving up the far side of the column. See?"

"Is he the one in the scarlet coat? On a black horse?"

"That's him!" a musketeer confirmed.

"What's on his shoulder?"

"Ah, you've spotted 'the little whore of Babylon.' "

"The what?"

"Rupert's pet monkey," said the corporal. "The Puritan preachers call it that. He also keeps a white poodle lapdog. It is trained to bark and jump high into the air at the name 'Charles', but to cock its leg up when his master says 'Pym'. Funny people these Germans."

By then the cavalry column had reached a point just beyond cannon range from the city. There the horsemen stopped and turned to face Gloucester. Prince Rupert and his staff rode to the front and also came to a halt. Thomas watched the Royalist officers conferring. Presently the ensign, still carrying the regimental colours, broke away from the group and rode towards Eastgate.

The ensign was a fair and dimpled youth with his long hair arranged in ringlets. Tall, pink feathers rose from his sweeping hat and there were layers of lace around his neck and wrists.

"My Lord, Prince Rupert," the ensign addressed the line of heads above the walls, "commands that you allow us to enter Gloucester in the name of the King."

"Tell him," Colonel Massy replied, "that we hold this city through Parliament for the King. Therefore we cannot surrender it to a foreign prince."

"Who are you, sir?" the ensign enquired, but Massey did not answer. "Whoever you are, sir," the cavalier went on after a pause, "I should warn you that my Lord, Prince Rupert does not take kindly to insults. The citizens of Cirencester tried to resist us and we took them by storm."

"They had no walls, no cannon," Massey pointed out, "nor the thousands of trained troops that are at my disposal. You waste your time, ensign. Go back and tell your master not to waste his."

The ensign took a long look at the line of heads before tugging the horse round and raking its sides with his spurs. As the animal sprang away towards the waiting Royalists, a ragged cheer ran along the city walls.

"What now?" Sergeant Major Pudsey asked Massey.

"If I were him," the colonel answered, "I would suggest a private parley on middle ground. Then I would make it a mixture of sweet reason and threats with some bribery in between. Which is why I do not intend to talk privately with Prince Rupert. Should the situation arise, two must go to represent the military and civil sides here. You, Henry and Councillor Jordan."

Edward Massey's forecast was uncannily accurate. The ensign returned to state that Prince Rupert requested a private parley with the military governor.

While Sergeant Major Pudsey was mounting his charger and Councillor Jordan a more docile mare, Colonel Massey watched Rupert of the Rhine moving forward to join the ensign. The German prince rode well as befits the leading cavalry commander of the age. The pet monkey was no longer on his shoulder.

The young prince had already packed his life with action. At the age of 14, he absconded from the University at Leyden to fight in the Low Countries. By the time he was 18, Rupert had impressed all who came in contact with him by his bravery and resourcefulness. Pudsey reflected on these traits as he rode out to meet such a formidable opponent.

"Keep to the city side of the prince and the ensign," he advised Jordan.

"You don't think . . .?"

"They may think I am the military governor and try to take me."

It was the first point Prince Rupert wished to establish.

"Who are you?" he brusquely addressed Pudsey. "Are you the commander here?"

"I am Sergeant Major Pudsey and second-in-command."

"Why is this?" Rupert's handsome face darkened. "I do not choose to speak with underlings."

"I am a soldier, sir. I obey orders."

"You will answer my questions. Who is the one with you?"

"Councillor Jordan, sir. A lawyer by profession."

"A lawyer!" Prince Rupert laughed before slapping his sword. "My law is by my side."

"In England," Tobias Jordan pointed out, "our laws are made by Parliament, which is why we are fighting you."

"Fighting? You never fought anyone in your life, lawyer. You never will. But enough of this." The Prince turned to Pudsey. "Let us talk as soldiers, Sergeant Major. I am giving you your last chance. Either you open the gates of Gloucester to me or I storm you."

"We cannot open a single gate, sir, without the permission of Parliament."

"Your London Parliament is a hundred miles away while Royalist Oxford lies in between and I am here. You see," Prince Rupert waved his right arm, "my main argument?"

"Our argument, sir, includes more men than yours, backed by high walls and cannon."

"I am well informed about you. You have but fifteen hundred soldiers of dubious quality and a few old guns. The citizens of Gloucester, crouching behind their crumbling walls with scythes and pitchforks, do not count."

"Then you will have to try us, sir."

"You are determined?"

"We are."

"So." Rupert transferred his gaze from Pudsey to the city walls, surveying them with the eyes of an expert. A full minute went by before the prince turned his horse and rode off without another word.

"What now, ensign?" Pudsey enquired.

"If I were you, Sergeant Major, I should go to see about your defences.

And to warn your commander that he was ill advised to insult a Prince. Particularly Prince Rupert."

"I shall do that, ensign." Pudsey gravely saluted the young man before leaving. As they rode towards Eastgate, Tobias Jordan asked,

"Will they attack?"

"I do not know, but Colonel Massey will. That is why he is our military governor and I am not. He is a man much like the one you have just met. Attuned to war."

"Rupert will not attack now," Massey confided in Pudsey after listening to an account of the parley. "However, do not pass on my opinion. I want every man to remain alert."

Several tense minutes went by then, without any preamble, the Royalist regiment turned away from Gloucester.

"The taking of Cirencester," Massey explained to the city fathers, "absorbed his energies and resources. Rupert also appreciates he is in predominantly Parliamentary countryside. My guess is he will make his way to Oxford and regroup with the King's forces."

"To return?" Alderman Pury voiced their thoughts.

"In strength," the military governor nodded.

The wind had been rising all day. It swept up the Severn Valley, beating on the hills. Copses were laid flat and branches snapped off trees. At Gloucester, people kept indoors listening to their creaking houses and fearful for roof tiles. Only the watchers on the walls remained out of doors and they crouched in corners, the sparks from their braziers streaming past them.

The Merrett household sat silent during the evening meal. This was because the master did not deign to commence any conversation. He glowered instead at an open door leading to the front hall.

A knock on the outer door was followed by Captain Pury letting himself into the house. Immediately Faith rose and went to him.

"Where's Thomas?" her brother asked without preamble. His helmet and breastplate glistened with raindrops.

"I sent him to put on more clothes."

"They'll soon be wet."

"Also a cloak."

"Between us, sister," Alan smiled, "we shall make a soldier of him."

"I do not want Thomas to become a soldier," Faith said fiercely, then added, "or you for that matter."

To change the subject, Captain Pury half turned and waved a greeting at Nathan through the doorway. The Puritan at the far end of the supper table nodded.

"What on earth do you see in him?" Alan whispered to his sister.

"He is a good man. A good husband to me. A good father to the twins. A good master to his apprentices — despite there being little or no work. Above all, Nathan is a man of peace."

"Peace?" Her brother smiled again, though sourly this time. "Such niceties could become liabilities in these troublesome days."

Their conversation was left unfinished by the appearance of Thomas Hobart. The lad had put on the cloak and secured it round his middle with a stout belt. Captain Pury said brusquely,

"Come on. We must not keep the colonel waiting."

Outside the raging storm had obliterated all sounds and smells. Blundering after the Captain, Tom discovered that the entire street was packed with horses and troopers standing beside them. Pury and he had to thrust their way between nervous animals and the sides of houses towards The Cross.

There, in the light of a fitful torch, Tom saw Colonel Massey talking to Under Sheriff Hill. They both held horses while Major Pudsey stood by. A soldier prodded Tom and said,

"Here's your pony, son."

Some roof tiles came clattering down, causing the mass of horses to shift uneasily. Men were tightening their grips and shouting 'Steady!' when the order came through to 'Mount up!' As he swung himself on to the back of his pony, Tom saw that Hill was riding beside Massey. The two men led the way towards Northgate.

Progress seemed impossible in such circumstances yet the horses settled down to a brisk trot. The wind being behind them helped, not least in keeping the stinging rain out of their eyes.

"All right?" Captain Pury shouted to Tom after they had splashed across a small brook without slackening pace.

"Yes sir. That was Down Hatherley brook. Where I used to live."

The officer did not speak again, leaving Thomas with his thoughts. How pleasant and permanent his childhood had seemed. His father a yeoman farmer. His mother a busy housewife. He longingly remembered a warm kitchen with hens and geese pecking about the yard outside and cattle in the meadows.

Tom tried not to think of his mother's death followed all too soon by that of his father. How Uncle Nathan Merrett had come to take him away from the silent farmhouse. Instead he concentrated on his riding and keeping close to Faith's brother. The wind was so strong it seemed to move the horsemen as one, sometimes sideways as well as forward.

After about an hour's riding, Colonel Massey called a halt in the lee of a wood. The men began to talk and were ordered to keep their voices down.

Within minutes the party was on the move again. Away from the sheltering trees, the storm seemed to have doubled in intensity. A horse stumbled and fell, its rider clattering on the ground. Someone asked,

"Are you hurt?"

"No, but the horse . . ."

"Either catch us up or go back," a gruff sergeant's voice summed up the situation. "We cannot wait."

Already Massey and Hill were a quarter of a mile away. Next came Captain Pury and Tom closely followed by the rest of the column. The wind roared around them.

Presently Tom saw a square of light ahead. As it grew in size, he identified the open door of a tall barn with lamps inside. The side of the barn loomed like a cliff next to the horsemen who were ordered to halt and wait. As they came to a standstill, Tom watched Massey and Hill ride into the barn and disappear. All the while, the wind shrieked and gusted around the waiting column.

"Why are we here?" another officer edged forward to ask Pury.

"I have heard talk of meeting with the under sheriff's brother."

"I did not know he had one."

"Massey knows. I wonder what he has in store for us tonight?"

"So do we all. Here they come."

The officer nodded towards the colonel and under sheriff riding from the barn. They were followed by a huge man mounted on an equally enormous horse. George Hill had the build of a bull, yet his brother was twice his size. To Tom and the rest of the company, it was as if they had been joined by a giant.

Now Colonel Massey and the newcomer led the way. They crossed roads and passed houses, but no lights shone and no one appeared. The wind was still at the soldiers backs and blowing harder. This was due to a steeply rising slope that fast became precipitous hillside. Horse after horse began to object to the difficult terrain.

"We must dismount," Tom heard Captain Pury mutter.

The order came a few moments later. Although his pony had remained obedient, Tom was relieved to slip from its back. He moved forward to the creature's head, at the same time whispering encouragement.

Due to the rugged nature of the ground, the soldiers allowed spaces to increase between them. The path they were following led ever upwards, narrowing under bulging rock faces against which the wind bounced. Each man and horse expected to be plucked off the track at any moment and hurled into the black void.

The crest of Cleeve was worst of all. Standing over a thousand feet above the Severn Valley, it threw the south wester upwards causing powerful swirls and eddies in its wake. Heavily armoured men and stout horses were shifted like leaves. Then, when it seemed impossible to hold on any longer, the wind suddenly ceased. The raiders were over the brow of the hill and in its shelter.

"Form up," came the order, "and mount."

Hastily the officers and men returned to their respective places behind Massey. Tom could see the colonel sitting as still as a statue while the troopers eased themselves into position. The wind continued to keen over their heads, but no longer buffeted them.

"Still with us, Tom?" Alan Pury enquired.

"Yes, sir."

"That was a blustery business. Here we go."

Their way lay downhill towards Winchcombe. Tom estimated the time to be after midnight. Certainly there was not a light to be seen. The horsemen appeared to be descending into a pool of darkness.

Yet, as they rode, the heavy clouds were breaking up above them. A star glimmered and then another. Gradually Tom was able to distinguish the line of hills and the battlements of a castle.

"Sudeley," he heard someone remark and another soldier muttered, "Surely Massey doesn't think we can take it?"

"Quiet there!" Captain Pury ordered.

The column came to a halt and the officers went forward for instructions. Presently Captain Pury returned to Tom's side and said,

"There are cattle beside those beech woods."

"Yes sir, I can see them."

"You are to remain by them until someone comes to you with further orders. If all goes well, it should be within the half hour. If not, you are to make your way back to Gloucester."

Tom had to repeat these directives before riding across parkland to a herd of heifers. By then the starlight was strong enough for him to turn and watch the column dividing into sections. The horsemen melted into the night and Tom was left alone.

When he slipped off his pony's back, the curious heifers immediately surrounded him. They kept inching forward though ready to back away at any movement. By standing quite still, Tom encouraged them to reach him. The first muzzle was within an inch of his hand when sounds of shooting and men shouting came from the castle.

Taking a firmer hold of his pony's bridle, Tom scanned the castle. The dark outline was being lit by flashes and lights began to appear at windows. The shouting increased and, added to it, were noises of doors being broken down and windows shattered. Flames shot skywards and Tom could see dark figures running past the fiery glow. As suddenly, the flames died down and all became silent.

Later a man strode across the meadow and called his name.

"Thomas Hobart, you are to report to Colonel Massey. We've taken the castle and he is in it. Go by the chapel and the side door. We'll look after your heifers for you."

More men appeared and they laughed at the last remark. Their laughter followed Tom as he led his pony towards Sudeley Castle. Unaccustomed to soldiering ways, he wondered what lay ahead. The scene meeting his eye was far different than he imagined.

First came temporary horse lines where he tethered the pony. Tom then approached the chapel, the inside of which blazed with candlelight and shook with heavy hammering. The noise was caused by Puritan soldiers breaking every statue and ornament. Looking in, Tom saw that the altar rails had been thrown to one side.

There was a small courtyard, formed between the chapel and castle, filled with men, women and children in various stages of night attire. Guards from Gloucester, holding loaded carbines and drawn swords, stood over them. A similar smaller group waited under guard within the side door.

Avoiding their gaze, Tom turned to a soldier he recognised and asked,

"Where do I find Colonel Massey? He sent for me."

"Yes," the soldier confirmed, "I have orders to pass you through. You follow this passage to the main hall. The colonel is in a room at the far side."

The passageway was panelled and there were paintings of richly dressed people at regular intervals. As Tom passed an open doorway, he glanced through it. The room contained a long table laden with food. Eating there and being served by two frightened maids were the monstrous Hill brothers.

The great hall beyond was crowded with officers and soldiers, including Captain Pury, searching through wooden chests. Faith's brother never glanced in his direction as Tom sidled past to the far door guarded by two musketeers.

"I am Thomas Hobart," he told them. "Colonel Massey sent for me."

"He is expecting you," a musketeer nodded and opened the door for him.

Inside, the room was fully furnished with tapestries as well as pictures on the panelled walls. All the candles had been lit and their flames were mirrored in the highly polished furniture. Colonel Edward Massey stood behind a table covered in papers, his helmet and a brace of cocked pistols. As Tom approached, he pulled a map over them.

"Do you think," Massey asked Thomas, "you can find your way back to Gloucester? On your own?"

"I'll try, sir."

"Trying is not good enough for me." The colonel's forefinger tapped the map sharply. "You are here at Sudeley Castle beside Winchcombe. To return to Gloucester, you must retrace your steps up the hill. It will be dawn by the time you reach the top of Cleeve and from there one can clearly see the tower of Gloucester cathedral."

"Yes sir."

"Do not attempt to descend the steep part of Cleeve Hill. When you reach the edge, go to the right where the slope becomes more gentle. You will find it an easier ride. On your way to Gloucester, avoid houses and people. If anyone challenges you, make up some story about visiting a sick relative."

"I understand, sir."

"On reaching Gloucester, you are to see Sergeant Major Pudsey. No one else. Tell him, we have taken Sudeley and are returning with carts. That is important. With carts," Massey stressed. "He is to bring two troops of horse and meet us by that barn — at Prestbury — the one we stopped at on our way here."

Thomas nodded and left when dismissed. In the hall, the officers were assembling piles of gold and silver ware. There was another pile of guns and swords. Men kept coming in with more and more booty. No one took any notice of Tom as he scurried along the passage to the courtyard.

On crossing the yard, Tom observed that the heifers were being herded beside the chapel. The gentle creatures were now extremely restless. It was all that a score of soldiers could do to restrain them. A heifer bellowed piteously as it was seized and dragged into the building. Glancing inside Tom saw that the chapel was drenched in blood from beasts being hacked to pieces on the altar.

A tremendous feeling of relief came over Tom when he rode away from Sudeley Castle. Presently parkland became hillside. Dawn seemed to have slipped out of the night and Tom was able to survey the Severn Valley from the top of Cleeve. Moreover the storm had washed the air so that every detail lay clearly discernible.

During the ride back, Tom saw no one because he avoided houses. Only when nearing Down Hatherley did he venture towards the old church and his parents' farm close by. The latter was now quite derelict. Someone had nailed a few boards across the doors and windows, while the barn stood open, its wide floor still wet from the rain.

On reaching Eastgate, Thomas asked to see Major Pudsey and was passed through to Greyfriars.

"You look tired, lad." Pudsey said. "Here, drink this." He handed Tom a goblet of wine.

The sweet red wine on Tom's empty stomach made him light-headed. He was glad of the invitation to sit down while telling his story and hoped the message was properly delivered. At the end of it, Sergeant Major Pudsey said,

"You have done your duty. Go home and get your head down. Sergeant!" he shouted and a trooper came running, "Two companies of horse to be ready in ten minutes. We ride to meet Colonel Massey and escort him back to Gloucester. He has taken Sudeley Castle."

The cheering and excitement echoed in Tom's ears as he threaded his way through alleys to the Merrett house in Westgate Street. There Uncle Nathan was loading timber and tools on to a cart, helped by a solitary apprentice. The rest were off elsewhere, helping to shift cannon.

"Good morning, Thomas," Nathan Merrett said from on top of the cart.

"Good morning, master," Tom politely replied.

"I am a master without apprentices." Nathan turned and adjusted the load leaving Tom to slink guiltily to his bed.

As 1643 wore on, the circle began to close round Gloucester. It did so slowly but surely.

To the citizens, it meant more soldiers coming and going. More earthworks to build. More cannon to shift. Mayor Wise formed his regiment of citizens. Apprentices enlisted or were away so often on other duties, that their masters lost control of them. Housewives, as ever, tried to maintain normality.

To Colonel Massey, it was a matter of military movements and dispositions. He was forever seeking information from passing soldiers, travelling tradesmen, anyone who could help fill in the picture of what was happening in the Civil War.

The picture was not a happy one for the Parliamentary cause. In the north, the Roundheads had been defeated by the Royalists. In the south, the King continued to occupy the centre of the chessboard at Oxford, with Princes Rupert and Maurice dominating the country between Gloucester and London.

There was more to come. The Cornish Royalists were swarming out of the West Country carrying all before them. Worse still, the Welsh army continued to menace Gloucester. After assembling at Coleford, it had moved to Highnam House, barely two miles from the city.

Massey had acted the moment the Welsh started to mass. Ignoring the Gloucester people, who could not take them seriously, he began to strengthen and garrison the old Bishop's Palace at Over. Even when this reached the maximum 200 men he could spare, Massey knew it to be insufficient. He needed help fast.

Thomas was on stand-by and chatting to another young galloper called

Simon when Sergeant Major Pudsey appeared in the doorway to Massey's office and barked,

"Simon, Thomas! In here."

They found Massey with two troopers, a sergeant and a corporal. As they were taking this in, Pudsey shut the door behind them and leaned against it. The colonel, without preamble, said,

"You are to pair off. A soldier and a boy. This is what needs to be done. As you know, the Welsh are at Highnam. Over two thousand of them, which is more than our entire force. I have no doubt we could attack them and win, but it would weaken our ability to hold Gloucester.

"Nevertheless, they have to be beaten. To do that I require the help of my old friend Major General Sir William Waller who is operating between here and Bristol. Our garrisons at Slimbridge and Eastington are in contact with him. I want you two," Massey nodded towards the sergeant and Simon, "to ride to Slimbridge, while you two go to Eastington.

"You may encounter enemy forces. You may have to split up. My message however must get through to General Waller. Tell him of our predicament. Ask if he can help. If he can, I shall join him at an agreed meeting point. Those are your orders. Go at once."

The journey to Eastington was uneventful. There the corporal and Thomas found the village surrounded by ditches, earthworks and sharpened spikes. A small company of soldiers, commanded by a lieutenant and augmented by armed villagers, met them. Suddenly the crowd parted as a tall Puritan preacher with a ravaged face came forward.

While the corporal was reporting to the lieutenant, Thomas recalled that Eastington was renowned for strong Puritan feelings. The preacher was, like the rest of his persuasion, sombrely dressed and wearing a plain felt hat. Two flaps dangled on either side of the hat. Thomas knew what they signified. Such flaps were worn by victims of ear slitting.

"I can lead you to Waller," said the Puritan. "I act as chaplain to his men. But I'll only take the boy."

At this point, Thomas thought the corporal would object. Instead the 'old soldier' turned to the lieutenant and asked,

"Your orders, sir?"

"Stay here," said the lieutenant.

Thus, after a short rest, Thomas found himself riding beside the Puritan towards Waller's camp hidden in the hills.

Their way south-westwards took them beneath the great Cotswold escarpment of heavily wooded slopes with the occasional outcrop of bare rocks. The journey alternately lay between open land and forest paths. Villages, even isolated cottages, were avoided.

Eventually they reached the centre of a valley, bounded by the wooded Cotswolds on the left and two equally wooded hills on the right, one before and the other behind them. All of a sudden, the situation changed when four groups of horsemen emerged from the trees, cutting off any chance of escape. The Puritan reined in his horse saying,

"Be still. They are Waller's men."

Thomas sat watching the troopers cantering towards them. All wore black rounded helmets with face bars, breast and back plates. Their leader, who was holding a pistol, suddenly lowered it and cried,

"Thomas! Thomas Hobart!" It was Lieutenant Richard Gwinnett. "You could not have brought me a more welcome messenger," Gwinnett said to the preacher as they made their way up a hill path to a high Cotswold valley.

"We but serve the Lord and our cause," the Puritan reminded him.

"Ah yes. The men will be glad to see you, sir. And General Waller to hear from his old friend Colonel Massey."

The high valley to which Gwinnett led them was well hidden and guarded. Once past the various sentries, Thomas saw an encampment containing hundreds of soldiers. Waller's men were fed and sustained by the surrounding villagers who had suffered so much from Royalist raiders. A humble woodman's hut, with a canvas awning added to provide increased coverage at the front, served as Waller's headquarters.

Major General Sir William Waller was then the most brilliant field commander Parliament possessed. Like Colonel Massey, he had learned his trade in Germany during the beginning of the Thirty Years War, serving in the same regiment as Robert Devereux, Earl of Essex and now Lord General for Parliament.

Through Essex's influence, Waller had been appointed commander of the Western Association comprising Somerset, Wiltshire, Shropshire, Worcestershire and Gloucestershire. A Devon man, he was well built with a round pleasant face belied by watchful eyes. Because Waller favoured raids during the hours of darkness, he became known as the Night Owl.

The major general, with a half circle of senior officers behind him, listened to the message Thomas had brought from Colonel Massey. On hearing it, he said, "We have to talk on this matter. Meanwhile my orderly will arrange sustenance for you."

The orderly led Tom and the preacher to a trestle table under the awning and indicated benches beside it. Presently he brought two wooden platters on which were pieces of cold fowl, also hunks of bread and cheese. A flagon of wine and two goblets followed. Thomas was ravenous, but had to wait while the Puritan gave lengthy thanks to God.

They had barely started to eat when the camp came astir. Several officers ran out of Waller's hut and began giving orders. A few moments later, a long line of horsemen clattered up the entrance path. Tom at once noticed that some of the horses were riderless and being led. Others had two men on their backs, those at the rear holding the ones in front. As these wounded men were released into the outstretched arms of their comrades, there were cries of,

"Surgeons! Chaplain!"

Leaving his meal untouched, the Puritan preacher from Eastington went to give comfort. Thomas also had to push away his platter. Some of the wounds made his stomach heave. At last the men were moved, the preacher returned to eat his food and the officers were back conferring with General Waller.

An hour went by, during which the sergeant and Simon, who had gone to Slimbridge, put in an appearance. They too were given a meal. As they ate, Sir William Waller came out of the hut and said,

"Here is my message to Colonel Massey. I shall help him. Tell him to meet me at Eastington tomorrow morning. As soon as possible after daybreak."

The return ride to Eastington appeared to go on forever. The wooded hills did not seem to move. Eventually the party reached the village where the grim preacher was replaced by a convivial corporal. There must have been some relaxation during the Puritan's absence.

The last lap to Gloucester continued with grey evening darkening into night. On one occasion horsemen were heard nearby. The sergeant waited until all was silent. Rain began to fall and Tom's pony shivered.

"Not long now," he said, patting its neck.

Eventually they passed into the city where the officer on duty sent them on to Sergeant Major Pudsey.

"Give me your message," said Pudsey. "The colonel is sleeping and I'll judge when to waken him with it."

They did so. It was brief enough yet the major was highly satisfied.

"Good. Go and rest," he said. "We shall meet General Waller at dawn."

The still night was followed by a day of movement. Peggy said there were soldiers out and about everywhere. Mrs Curtis had heard that Colonel Massey was back in the city issuing a stream of orders. The committee of defence met and later the sheriff's men went round informing every householder he would have to billet double the amount of soldiers in the near future.

"Six now," Nathan grumbled, "instead of three."

"Which means eighteen shillings," Faith pointed out, "instead of nine. If they bring me their daily rations — a pound of meat and two of bread — we shall all eat well."

Outside the rain had started again and Westgate Street became a slimy stream.

During the evening, groups of musketeers and pikemen were assembled at The Cross before marching to the Severn bridge and causeway. Later troopers came leading their horses. Citizens watched from doorways as the soldiers squelched in the mud. The wind was rising and driving the rain.

"Tonight," Nathan Merrett told his household, "we shall pray. The women upstairs. We men downstairs." He had three of his apprentices with him, including Thomas.

The entire city prayed. Everyone also listened, but could hear only rain water running down the gutters. Around midnight, the wind rose to gale force. It lashed the rain against windows making those within think of their menfolk at Highnam.

Nathan Merrett held his Bible before him but had ceased reading it. Across the table, two of his apprentices were asleep, heads on their arms. Thomas felt his eyelids drooping. Soon he too would have to succumb. Suddenly he heard shouting.

"Victory, victory!" the shouting came nearer. "We've beaten the Welsh."

Nathan and Thomas rushed to the street door and flung it wide open. A man came towards them, weaving from side to side.

"Victory!" he kept informing the householders, who caught hold of him then pushed him onwards. "Massey and Waller have won."

"What happened?" Nathan too seized the man and almost lifted him off the ground.

"Victory!" the man kept on shouting. His breath reeked of drink and the Puritan released him in disgust.

"Uncle," said Thomas. "I am known by the soldiers. Let me go and find out more."

"Very well," Nathan agreed.

Tom immediately raced along Westgate Street. The guards at the gate had been joined by others from the walls and a crowd of citizens. Soon Thomas learned the welcome news and more messengers were arriving with further information.

They told how that evening Major General Waller and his full force crossed the river by Framilode ferry. On the stroke of midnight they had stormed the Welsh around Highnam House. At the same time, Massey led his attack from the Gloucester side. It was a classic pincer movement and it worked.

As the messengers returning to Gloucester put it, over 1500 jabbering Welshmen were surrounded and had surrendered. Carts were needed to collect their arms, food supplies and other spoils of war. Thomas returned and told his uncle.

"Praise the Lord of Hosts," said Nathan, "and the strong arms of the righteous."

At daybreak, Tom slipped out once more. This time grim scenes met his eye. The wounded were being brought in and directed to certain households by John Dorney, the town clerk. Grimmer still, several dead bodies had to be handed over to mourning relatives.

Moving away, Tom saw a group led by Under Sheriff Hill holding stout staves. When the Welsh prisoners arrived between lines of musketeers and pikemen, Hill and his cronies took over. They drove the hundreds of dejected losers towards the church of St Mary de Lode. Since its long abandonment, the building had been used for storage and lately to stable horses. Now over 1500 men were crammed inside.

For the next ten days, while the rest of Gloucester rejoiced, Hill's men kept watch over the prisoners. Money was provided by the committee of defence for their sustenance, but the jailers drank most of it. The only food that went into the church were turnip tops and old cabbage leaves in buckets of dirty water. Gradually the prisoners fell silent in their stench.

Before being released, the Welsh swore an oath never again to fight against Gloucester. Afterwards, Hill made them scrub out the church and only then were they allowed to depart. By that time much else was happening. While Waller's men enjoyed a well earned rest, Massey led the city forces to take Tewkesbury.

Massey took Tewkesbury and, with Waller's further help, Hereford. Their successes however attracted the Royalists' attention. Prince Maurice and his superbly trained troops were sent against them. Although Maurice lacked Rupert's dash, he made up for this by thoroughness and tenacity. As spring turned to summer, the Parliamentary forces were pushed back to Gloucester. Their whole campaign was wasted.

Those in charge became increasingly concerned. The city fathers and military commanders spent sleepless nights. The soldiers and citizens knew something was wrong. Rumours from the faint-hearted reached the most resolute. A tentative peace party was formed by the Puritans with Tobias Jordan in the background. Meanwhile, Sir William Waller informed the committee,

"I cannot remain here. The King at Oxford is using two large cavalry forces. Maurice in the Midlands and Rupert to the south west. The former still harries us. The latter is menacing Bristol. I must go there for, if Bristol falls . . ." he left the rest unsaid.

"Let us not surmise about the future," said Pury. "What about now?" I assume you are leaving Colonel Massey and his men here?"

"Yes sir," Waller responded. "They are pledged to you by Parliament."

Next morning the major general left Gloucester with his seasoned troopers. Grim-faced they rode out of Southgate towards Bristol. The city guards watched until they vanished in the heat haze. It was another sweltering day.

The days that followed were hotter still. Alderman Pury felt the council chamber was becoming a furnace. Despite opening every window, the heat seemed to increase rather than disperse. Perhaps this was because every visitor, every newcomer, every messenger gave him bad news. The Parliamentary cause was like a shred of paper burning round the edges.

In early July, the Battle of Lansdown Hill, three miles north of Bath, was fought. It was bloody yet indecisive. A week later came another bloodier battle, this time at Roundway Down near Bristol. There Waller's tired men were all but destroyed by the Royalist cavalry.

Mid-July brought reports of Prince Rupert leaving Oxford at the head of a considerable force comprising fresh regiments of foot and horse. He headed for Bristol, contemptuously shouldering the remnants of Waller's troops towards Gloucester. The city garrison was horrified when the once successful major general crept in with a few men and many more wounded in carts.

"Dear friend," Waller said to Massey when they were alone, "you are on your own. I am finished. I must return to London and report my failures. They deserve to have my head and, to tell the truth, I no longer mind."

As before, John Dorney allocated the wounded to selected households. Every house in Gloucester was full and, to set an example, council members took more than their share. Mrs Pury was tearful to learn that her husband had accepted four badly wounded officers.

"I suppose," she complained, "you'll be wanting them to have my bedroom?"

"Of course not. We have plenty of other rooms. These men have been fighting for you."

"Not fighting for me," Hortense Pury objected. "If you had acted as peacemaker between Pym and the King, which I advised at the time, this would never have happened. I am sure Mrs Pym would not allow such cases in her house."

"You really must help me, Hortense — as Faith has done."

"Ah yes, Faith!" Mrs Pury cried. "She will know what to do."

Faith brought Peggy to assist her, leaving Mrs Curtis with the twins. It was a case of making each wounded man comfortable, then leaving it to nature and the Lord. Rough pallets were replaced by bedding and blood soaked bandages with fresh linen.

One of the officers died before Faith reached him and had to be removed. Another had his upper right arm severed, also a deep cut between his ribs. The old bandages were crusted and reluctant to come away. While Faith worked gently at them, Peggy sponged the anguished face. A candle barely illuminated this dismal scene.

"It's him!" Peggy suddenly exclaimed.

"Who?" Faith concentrated on removing the last of the dirty dressing.

"Lieutenant Gwinnett. Poor man, surely he suffered enough the first time?"

Though the words registered, Faith was looking at what lay beneath the old wad of cloth. It had covered a stump and the chest wound. Both were ghastly.

"Thank the Lord," said Faith, "he is unconscious. Peggy, there's an old soldier downstairs who knows more about wounds than I do. Please go and get him."

The soldier was not much help.

"I'd say," he said, "you've another goner. Like the one we've removed."

"No." Faith was surprised at the firmness in her voice.

The old soldier rubbed his chin thoughtfully.

"In Germany, they favour irons from the fire for such wounds. In the Low Countries, hot tar."

"No." Faith said again.

In the end, as in the Bible, she applied oil and wine before binding up the wounds with clean cloths. Later, after seeing to the other two patients, Faith returned and sat by Richard Gwinnett's bedside. She was still there when Nathan arrived.

"See who it is," said Faith. "He has turned up again."

To her surprise, Nathan did not reply at once. Instead he took the candle and brought it nearer to the lieutenant's face. For a long time, the Puritan studied the wounded man's features. Eventually he whispered,

"The Lord doth try us sorely."

"Doth try him."

"I am no good here," Nathan went on. "Not like you Faith showing so much charity. Your father below has asked me to join him in prayer. We may help by faith and hope, though the greatest of all is charity."

The long night crept by. Despite her concern and sitting in an uncomfortable position, Faith fell asleep. She woke with a start, stiff and alarmed. The candle was out, but the first faint light of morning shone on Richard Gwinnett's face. Searching the face, Faith saw that the suffering had left it. Alarmed she looked for signs of life and found he was still breathing. Gwinnett was unconscious, but he would live.

'Though not,' Faith thought, 'to fight again'. She then went and attended the other two officers.

The defeat and departure of Major General Sir William Waller depressed those who remained in the city. It was as if a great axe hung over the garrison and inhabitants. All their efforts had come to nought. The Midlands had reverted to the Royalists. The King's armies ruled the West

Country. Even the perfidious Welsh were on the move again. Only Bristol and Gloucester stood like large and small rocks respectively in a raging sea.

"Bristol will sustain us," people told each other. "After London, it is the premier port and city loyal to Parliament. We are connected to Bristol by water as well as land. By sticking together, the King will never defeat us."

When he heard these arguments in public, Colonel Massey would agree. In private however, speaking to his officers or the committee of defence, Massey expressed more realistic views.

"Following Waller's defeat at Roundway Down, Bristol lies militarily unprotected. We must continue to look after our own defences. For this purpose, I am withdrawing the small garrisons at Eastington and Slimbridge. We need the men and their weapons. The villagers will either have to join us or fend for themselves."

"Colonel Massey is right," Alderman Pury summed up the discussion. "We are thirty miles from Bristol and one hundred from London. Sooner or later, the main Royalist forces will turn on us. Try to take us. It is an ominous thought."

The last days of July slipped swiftly by. No news reached Gloucester, either from Bristol or elsewhere. Massey sent out scouts, but they quickly returned. It appeared that the whole of the county was swarming with the King's soldiers. The nobility in their country houses were reasserting themselves and humble villagers falling silent. Small boys in Cheltenham had actually thrown stones at one of Massey's troopers.

Then late in the afternoon of the 26th July, a farmer from Chipping Sodbury with relatives in Gloucester arrived at Southgate. He began by babbling about his farmhorses being commandeered by the Royalists, then how he had found one left and ridden direct to the city on it.

"But what of your news, man?" asked the duty sergeant.

"If there is any news," his captain pointed out, "it must first be related to the military governor. That is a standing order."

"Whoever hears," said the farmer, "will not care for it."

The news that came to Massey, was relayed to the committee, then spread rapidly round the city, causing utter despondency. Prince Rupert with his fresh forces from Oxford had stormed and taken Bristol. The farmer told how the remaining Parliamentary horsemen had been chased across the Bristol Downs and into the Avon Gorge.

"The Lord has left us to the last," said Mayor Wise.

"And naked to our enemies," Tobias Jordan added.

"No," Colonel Massey said vehemently, "not naked. We have made preparations and they shall continue. With your permission," he said, "I must ride round the city to reassure citizens and soldiers alike. To tell them that we have walls where Bristol had not. To remind them our cannon is in place and our garrison intact. Above all, we are of one mind."

"While you are doing that," Alderman Pury said, "we shall send messengers to London asking for military aid. Six at least for the King's men lie thick in between."

For the rest of that day, while six experienced riders left in turn from Eastgate, Colonel Massey exhorted everyone to keep calm and of good cheer. The walls and earthworks they had been strengthening were far superior to anything at Bristol. Moreover Gloucester had sufficient cannon and the production of gunpowder was rising.

"We have more than enough musketeers, pikemen and other fighting men," Massey kept saying to the citizens. "Line the walls with us and your city will be impregnable. Prince Rupert knew the first time he could not ride over us. His chances become less with each passing day. With every stone you add. With every sackful of earth you carry.'

'Lord,' Edward Massey prayed between these exhortations, 'help me to convince them when I am not sure myself.'

July turned to August with no more firm news reaching Gloucester. This respite was used in many ways. The citizens managed to bring in an early harvest. The committee of defence sought to improve billeting arrangements and Mrs Pury took the opportunity to move the wounded out of her home. Richard Gwinnett, who fortunately was on the mend, was shifted to an attic room in Tobias Jordan's house.

For his part, Colonel Massey continued to work on the city defences. He kept his officers, men and civilian helpers hard at it, yet they recognised the concern of their commander. Cannon, muskets and pistols were tested. Swords were sharpened and pikes ground to needle points.

On the first Friday in August, a Royalist captain was seen approaching Eastgate. He halted when challenged and, indicating a letter in his gauntlet, stated it was for Alderman Pury. Four troopers with carbines levelled went out to collect it. When Pury received the letter, he opened it in full view of the committee and read out its contents. He then passed the missive round the table commenting,

"The usual persuasion for surrendering our city. Note the promises of preferment alternated by threats about the might of the King's army."

"Is an answer required?" asked John Dorney who had not yet read the letter.

"By Sunday," Pury replied, "though you may minute that we shall not do so."

Throughout the weekend, country people kept arriving at the city gates. Those coming on Saturday afternoon told of Royalist forces on the march from Bristol. Massey immediately sent out scouts who confirmed the reports. By nightfall, the vanguard of the King's army was within ten miles of Gloucester.

An uneasy night followed. The dawn watch saw no soldiers, but during

Sunday morning, church services were interrupted by further disquicting news. A brigade of Royalist horse had appeared, as if from nowhere, on Tredworth Field.

"This is the time," said Massey, "to send out a strong party."

"To take on a whole brigade?" Pudsey raised his eyebrows.

"In another direction," the colonel smiled. "Out of Southgate towards Wotton and back by Upton. Under Captains Harcus, Blunt and Pury I think. The object of the exercise is to learn if more Royalists are on the move, to attack if in sufficient strength and to take prisoners if possible."

Three hours later, the raiding party returned with ten prisoners and news of considerable enemy forces everywhere. As Captain Harcus reported,

"We had several fights on our hands. There are Royalists gathering at Tuffley, Matson and Brookthorpe."

From that hour onwards, the walls of Gloucester were fully manned night and day. Massey's men lined the ramparts and earthworks with muskets, pikes and cannon. At each of the four gatehouses, two hundred horsemen stood by and, as if these preparations were not enough, the colonel decided on an inner line of defences.

The Merrett household was involved early on the Monday morning. Mrs Curtis arrived before her usual time weeping piteously. It took minutes before Faith could get some sense out of her.

"My house," Mrs Curtis kept saying. "My only home."

In the end, Faith and Thomas accompanied the widow to her house which stood within the south wall. As they approached, the reason for Mrs Curtis's upset became clear. Her belongings were piled in the street and an endless chain of men were carrying baskets of earth into the building. Already they had filled the downstairs rooms from floor to ceiling.

"What are you doing?" Faith asked a man she knew.

"It is a shame, Mistress Merrett," the man paused for a moment, "but the wall is weak here. So we have orders to fill all the houses along this side, making them solid to their rooftops. After that, we must pack the space between the filled houses and the wall itself, again to roof level. In that way, the thickness will be threefold."

"Who has ordered this?"

"The committee of defence after an application by the military governor. Your father signed the order last night and we began work at first light. I can understand Mrs Curtis's grief."

"Can you spare two men to help take her possessions to my house?"

"Certainly Mrs Merrett."

"Thank you," Faith said. "Come Mrs Curtis," she put her arm round the still weeping woman. "Let us look on the bright side. Your property will remain intact whatever happens to the rest of us. In the meantime, you shall have a room with all your belongings."

Tom slipped away soon after Mrs Curtis was settled in the Merrett household. News had come through of Royalists plundering the tiny village of Tuffley. He arrived at the gatehouse as Captain Pury and Lieutenant Pierce set out with forty musketeers and a few horse. Later he heard their approach caused the Royalists to fall back on Brookthorpe where a fierce skirmish took place.

Initially, several of the enemy were killed and one taken prisoner. Then Royalist cavalry counter attacked and captured a Parliamentarian soldier. The city force was obliged to make a fighting withdrawal and also fortunate in being relieved by Colonel Massey leading out a strong troop of horse.

"Edward," Pudsey said afterwards, "you should not have endangered yourself."

"I was the nearest and it had to be done quickly."

"Nevertheless . . ."

"Oh come now, Henry. There is worse news. The King's main force has reached Berkeley and his artillery is on its way from Cirencester. I also saw large groups of dragoons along the Cotswold skyline."

Another uneasy night followed with messengers bringing in vital pieces of information.

"Preparations," one said, "are being made by Lady Bridgeman to entertain the King in her Painswick home."

"Lord Chandos," said another, "has arrived at and eaten in Lady Guise's house by Brockworth."

When the latter news was relayed to Massey, he sent out another raiding party — Chandos being more vulnerable than the King and Brockworth nearer to the city. The party was made up of a hundred musketeers and pikemen flanked by fifty horse. It left by Eastgate and had only reached Barnwood when it was attacked. During the running fight, a Royalist officer was killed.

As before, reinforcements came up to exact revenge. The fight continued all the way back to Gloucester. It was finally resolved when Pudsey galloped out leading fifty more horsemen.

"Now you have endangered yourself," Massey remarked on Pudsey's return. The sergeant major however was not amused.

"Everywhere's swarming with Royalists," he reported. "There are thousands of them, all heading this way."

For the rest of the day, company after company of marching men and troop after troop of horse soldiers could be seen converging on Gloucester. The defenders on the battlements observed long columns wending their respective ways from Oxford and Bristol, Wales and the Midlands. Bright coated cavalry poured down the Cotswolds hills. Lines crossed and colours blended, their kaleidoscopic movements continuing into the dusk. By nightfall, the city was encircled by camp fires.

The hours of darkness seemed never ending for the defenders braced to receive the shock of an attack at any moment. None came, yet when the morning of Thursday 10th August dawned, the watchers along the walls noted further forces were still arriving. Never in their lives had the citizens of Gloucester seen so many soldiers. The fields they so recently harvested were packed with enemy troops.

The morning hours appeared longer than those of the night. The King's army worked to a plan and was in no hurry. Each company, moving to its predetermined position, was led by a captain followed by an ensign carrying the colours. Then came musketeers in order of march, flanked by pikemen, with drummers beating out the required paces.

Next the artillery trains lumbered past, gun upon gun. The heavy cannon were pulled by eight horses in pairs, the lighter by four. Great waggons followed them laden with powder barrels and sacks of shot, ladles and ramrods, ropes and pulleys. Still more carts carried tents, rations and other necessities of war.

The most eyecatching sight was the cavalry whose regiments of five hundred strong moved as one. The heavy cavalry wore shot proof armour, barred helmets, studded gauntlets and long padded boots. The light cavalry had less armour, but the same deadly combination of weapons comprising swords, carbines and a brace of pistols apiece.

Prominent were the red coated dragoons who rode for mobility then dismounted to fight on foot. They were used as shock troops to seize and hold key positions until the arrival of the main body. Their swords had cut-and-thrust blades for close fighting.

Towards mid-morning, when all seemed assembled, the King's own soldiers, numbering 6000 strong and more superbly equipped than the rest, arrived at the foot of Robinswood Hill. They manoeuvred from loose order to close formation, then marched across Tredworth Field to within a quarter of a mile from the south wall of the city. After them came a further 2000 horse soldiers who went on to face the north side.

Lookouts, reporting to Colonel Massey, told of still more Royalists arriving from the directions of Tewkesbury and Cheltenham. Throughout the morning also, Welsh forces assembling west of the Severn swelled in numbers. It was as if they had never been defeated and humiliated by the Gloucester garrison. While spreading along the river bank, they shouted threats of an early revenge.

By noon, the Royalist ring was not only complete and solid, it stood in considerable depth. After viewing most of this menacing circle, Colonel Massey rejoined the city fathers on the wall overlooking Tredworth. From there they watched the King's pavilion being erected. The sound of mallets rang in the air. Sumptuous scarlet and gold cloth billowed then tautened as cords were pulled tight. Simultaneously, cavalry commanders were seen to leave their regiments and ride towards the pavilion.

"There," said Pudsey, "is our old friend Prince Rupert."

"With Prince Maurice beside him," Massey nodded.

"Here comes the King's coach," said Mayor Wise. "See the plumed horses and the coat-of-arms."

Cheers rippled along the Royalist lines as King Charles the First — tiny and dainty — stepped from his coach on to red carpets covering the grass. The front of the pavilion was open and Thomas Hobart, who had kept close to Massey, heard the Colonel mutter,

"The stage is set and the play about to begin."

"Sir," Alderman Pury addressed his military commander, "we have but 1500 soldiers and 500 armed citizens. A bare two thousand. From your experience, how many would you care to estimate King Charles has brought against us?"

"I have already estimated," said Massey, "and it is upwards of 30,000."

PART TWO

THE BELEAGURED CITY

"Heralds," said Mayor Dennis Wise. "One I recognise as the Somerset herald, though not the other."

"They must be given entry," Councillor Tobias Jordan said, "and not molested in any way. The rules of war . . ."

The rest of the council members nodded while Colonel Massey reflected there were no real rules when fighting one's fellow men.

At a nod from Alderman Pury, the gates were opened so the two heralds did not have to alter the pace of their horses. They seemed to have all the time in the world and were oblivious of sightseers. As the heralds rode along Eastgate to The Cross, the crowd followed. Masses of people pushed down the street behind them, also came out of side roads and alleyways.

On reaching The Cross, both heralds sat perfectly still for some time. At last the crowd was solid and silent. Only then did the Somerset herald take the proclamation from the top of his gauntlet and unfold it. People at the back heard him clearing his throat, then he spoke in a deep, far-reaching voice.

"I am empowered to read you this proclamation from His Majesty, King Charles the First.

"Out of our tender compassion to our city of Gloucester and that it may not be destroyed by our army, which we cannot prevent if we are compelled to attack, we have personally come here.

"We are pleased to let all the inhabitants and all the soldiers within the walls know that if they immediately submit themselves and deliver our city to us, we are contented to pardon everyone without exception.

"In the word of a King, we do assure them they will not receive the least damage or prejudice by our army to their persons and property, instead we would appoint a moderate governor and garrison to reside with you for the ease and security of our city.

"But if they should neglect our offer of grace and favour, and compel us by the power of our army to reduce this place — which by the help of God we shall easily and shortly be able to do — they will then have to thank themselves for all the calamities and miseries befalling them.

"To this message we expect a clear and positive answer within two hours, hereby giving safe passage for those coming to and returning from us, and do order all the officers and soldiers of our army to let them so pass."

"I would ask," the Somerset herald addressed Mayor Wise, whom he knew, "to secure this proclamation openly on The Cross, so all may read it."

"The proclamation does not say so," Alderman Pury replied for the committee of defence, "and therefore we do not permit it."

"Give me your message," Wise held out his hand, "and we will return our answer in due course."

"Within the stipulated time," The herald handed him the document.

"Colonel," Pury turned to Massey, "See the heralds from the city, then join us with Sergeant Major Pudsey."

Ten minutes later, the two officers knocked on the door of the council chamber and were let in by John Dorney. The King's proclamation lay in front of Alderman Pury like a drawn sword. Massey saw that the councillors were tense and nervous. For a moment he wondered if they would submit, until Alderman Pury informed him to the contrary.

"We are of one mind, that is to continue with our opposition to the King. He speaks of his word, but what is it worth? We know what would happen to us if we opened the gates and laid down our arms. By nightfall we would be imprisoned and tomorrow dead."

"What we do not know," Mayor Wise looked directly at Massey, "is our ability to resist such a force as the King has brought against us. I play at soldiers with my town regiment, but you are a professional. You and Sergeant Major Pudsey here. Tell us, reassure us on our power to resist."

"Three quarters of the troops out there," Colonel Massey answered, "are useless for a siege. For a siege, one needs sappers, digging and mining equipment."

"There are reports," said Tobias Jordan, "that miners from the Forest of Dean will be helping the King."

"Yes, I know," Massey answered. "Therefore we have to stop them and the only way to do so is by frequent sorties. I have already made plans for these. Whatever happens, sieges take time, during which the besiegers outside are at risk. By now Parliament will know of our predicament and Essex will act."

"And you," Pury looked at Major Pudsey. "Are you satisfied as to our all-round defences?"

"They are strong and daily becoming stronger." Pudsey answered. "They will be manned round the clock. Whenever the King attacks, we shall retaliate."

"Could Rupert overrun us?" Jordan asked nervously.

"No, neither Prince Rupert nor Prince Maurice — or anyone else. Their cavalry is useless even if a breach were made. Then it would be a matter of hand-to-hand fighting."

"We must see to it," Pury did not raise his voice, "that no breach is made. That the walls are fully manned. That they become stronger. We are still of one resolve and must now compile a suitable answer to the King. John, would you help me here?"

"As always, sir," Dorney replied.

"I was thinking of legal suitability," said Pury, "and the right words. No doubt the King will publish his proclamation and our reply. The printers are busy, I have heard say, at Oxford. There is also the verdict of history to consider. What we do here this afternoon could be weighed and judged in centuries to come."

"Well, sir," said John Dorney, who had been making a few notes, "we must bring Parliament into the matter. The King, you will have noticed, made no mention of Parliament in his proclamation."

"A good point!" Dennis Wise agreed.

"Our oaths are to King and Parliament," Alderman Pury nodded. "To both houses in fact. Let us say so in a few words."

The town clerk drafted three sentences, then read them to the committee.

"We the inhabitants, magistrates, officers and soldiers within this garrison of Gloucester, return our humble reply to His Majesty's gracious message.

"We do keep this city according to our oaths for the use of His Majesty and of his royal posterity.

"We conceive ourselves wholly bound to obey the commands of His Majesty — as signified by both Houses of Parliament — and are resolved by God's help to keep this city accordingly."

"Admirable," Pury said. "Make the necessary copies with the best one going to the King."

While John Dorney was writing and re-writing the sentences, Wise asked,

"Who goes to the King? Should I as mayor, accompanied by the sheriff, return our reply?"

"What do you think?" Pury asked Massey.

"I think not," the colonel answered. "I contend it should be Major Pudsey and Councillor Jordan as before. Anyone more senior they might delay."

Once again Pudsey and Jordan rode out as envoys.

"This time," said Pudsey, "keep beside me."

There was a wide space, the width of cannon fire, between the city walls and the outskirts of the King's army. This space was deserted though not all open. Here and there were houses, a mixture of humble cottages and country homes of the well-to-do. They now stood empty, their gardens unattended.

All too soon, Pudsey and Jordan reached the first line of troops. There they had to wait while officers learned who they were and passed the message back. This happened on six occasions, thereby making their progress a slow one. A sergeant major was assigned to Pudsey and a provost to Jordan.

"We know each other," said the Royalist major.

"Indeed we do." Pudsey replied.

"I find it hard seeing you on the wrong side."

"And I you."

Tobias Jordan said nothing to his appointed companion.

They had reached within a hundred paces of the King's pavilion, but were not destined to cross that last strip of Tredworth Field over which children had so recently played. Between the emissaries and the crown were staff officers and generals, courtiers and noblemen, all bowing and scraping towards the Royal presence.

Following a flutter of movement from the pavilion, nobles addressed generals who in turn spoke to staff officers. Eventually the Royalist major with Pudsey was called away. On his return, he asked for Gloucester's reply.

"Here." Pudsey handed over the document, which Dorney had meticulously prepared. The major took and passed it to a more senior officer leaving Pudsey and Jordan in the midst of the swarming camp.

"Keep still," Pudsey said from the corner of his mouth, for Jordan's nervousness seemed to have affected the horse.

"I have wet myself." Tobias Jordan confessed.

'You would,' Pudsey thought as he tried to see past the lines of Royalists into the pavilion. The King was difficult to distinguish, being so small. It was easier to watch the knot of courtiers around him, moving as their master moved.

Nearly an hour went by, then the front of the pavilion was abruptly closed. Something was happening. Officer after officer was leaving; mounting and galloping back to their regiments. The crowd was dispersing and through it, riding towards Pudsey and Jordan, came Prince Rupert of the Rhine. A smile spread over the prince's face on seeing Pudsey.

"I know you, sergeant major and you too," he said to Tobias Jordan. "The able second-in-command and the pettifogging lawyer. The King does not deign to answer the insulting message from your rebellious city. You may go back and tell them that."

"Yes, sir," Pudsey bowed slightly while Jordan was already tugging his horse round.

"One moment more," Prince Rupert was amused. "Sergeant major, inform Colonel Massey that I too know a great deal about siege warfare, as he and the rest of you will soon find out. I would advise you and Massey to leave that nest of traitors and join me. Good officers are always welcome in my regiments.

"As for you, lawyer," Rupert moved closer to Jordan, "you must begin preparing yourself for a rope round your throat." The prince sniffed, then touched a perfumed handkerchief to his nose before adding, "When that happens, you'll do more than wet yourself."

Rupert of the Rhine rode away laughing and his staff laughed with him. Pudsey noticed that the Royalist troops were parting, to allow safe conduct back to the city gate. He growled at the petrified Jordan.

"Come on, man."

Slowly they rode between the impassive soldiers, Pudsey his head held high and Jordan visibly trembling. When they were past the outer line, the experienced sergeant major said,

"Now you see what war is like. If only you knew, you politicians would not keep forcing it on us."

It was peaceful in the zone between the two forces. Peaceful that is until men with torches came running out of the city. Jordan looked startled, while Pudsey knew the exact nature of their orders from Massey.

"They are to burn every house out here," he explained, at the same time spurring his horse to a brisk trot. "So that none can be used by the enemy. As outposts for sharpshooters."

"I understand." Tobias Jordan nodded then said, "I drew up the deeds for many of these houses."

"Faster!" Pudsey cried, looking over his shoulder. "The Royalists are starting to occupy the outer suburbs of Barton Street."

As if to confirm this, musket fire began crackling from either side, followed by the deeper roar of cannon. Tobias Jordan was never so thankful as when the city gates opened and closed behind him. Ignoring Pudsey and everyone else, he rode straight to his tall, narrow house, left his horse unattended and retired to his bedchamber.

A few minutes later, Mrs. Jordan came to the foot of the attic stairs and called,

"Lieutenant Gwinnett! Can you help me? My husband has a fever."

Laboriously, Gwinnett climbed down and accompanied the woman. A glance at Tobias told him what was wrong.

"What he needs and I shall give to him is a goblet of mulled wine."

"Wine?" the Puritan's wife recoiled.

"Yes, get it and I shall give it to him."

Jordan gulped down the wine then began crying on Gwinnett's wounded shoulder. It hurt the Lieutenant, who did not, however, move.

Colonel Massey's headquarters at Greyfriars was the scene of constant activity throughout the siege. Officers came and went at all hours of the day and night. Sergeant Major Pudsey handled military matters and John Dorney, who had taken the place of Tobias Jordan, looked after city liaison and civilian subjects.

Thomas Hobart's position remained unchanged. He could not ride beyond the city walls, but Massey had constant messages for all parts of the defence network. One moment Tom would be racing to Eastgate or Westgate, the next climbing the old castle steps or running breathlessly along the northern embankments.

Information came in thick and fast. The enemy had already started digging trenches across Gaudy Green. Royalist horsemen were probing the riverside marshes and the city's outlying system of earthworks. As for the Welsh, they were taking pot shots over the Severn.

"The water pipes from Robinswood Hill into the town conduits," Dorney reported to Massey, "have been cut."

"As we expected," the colonel retorted. "Most citizens will use their own rainwater tubs and more wells must be dug."

"What about the cornmills powered by water?"

"We have plenty of spare horses. It'll be a way of exercising them. Have that furniture fellow construct horse-driven devices. You know the man. Pury's son-in-law, I believe."

"Yes, Nathan Merrett."

"Well, don't let him make anything fancy." Colonel Massey turned to more pressing matters.

Such activity went on throughout the night. Thomas slept, was shaken awake, ran with messages and fell asleep again. Officers and men catnapped around him. It grew quieter during the early hours yet Colonel Massey did not sleep. This was the time for gis spies.

They reported one after another — water-rat men, tinkers and thieves. They had crept through enemy lines collecting an assortment of information like pieces of a puzzle. Massey paid for these according to their worth. Some he argued over. Others he rewarded with unexpectedly high sums.

The King's Lord General Ruthen had placed his headquarters in the fields behind Lanthony. Sir Jacob Ashley was occupying a house at the lower end of Barton Street. The cavalry princes were back on the heights, their horselines ranged between Haresfield and Prinknash. As for the King, he was at Matson House, his personal guards deep around him.

A more official report came at the fourth hour from Captain Harcus at Southgate. The sounds of digging had gone on all night. Enemy trenches were stretching towards the city. Could he attack?

Colonel Massey stormed out there. "Since when do you need my permission to attack the enemy?" he demanded of Harcus.

"My apology and thank you, sir," the young captain grinned. "I have a hundred men ready and waiting."

"Then use them, sir. This minute."

With pistols primed and swords drawn, the force slid away into the darkness. Moments later shots rang out, followed by yells. Then came shrieks mingled with triumphant shouts. Soldiers began running back to the city carrying picks and shovels. Eventually, Captain Harcus reappeared to report,

"Not a man lost, sir."

"As it should be," Massey smiled when saying this. "Mark my word, they'll counterattack at daybreak."

It was dawn when Thomas ran on to the parapet and tugged at Massey's sleeve.

"Sir, sir, I have to tell you there are attacks at Eastgate and towards the Barbican."

"Keep your head down, boy," Colonel Massey actually put his hand on top of Tom's head and pushed him downwards, "while I attend to them."

The day which had started briskly, was soon one of feverish activity. All round the city, the Royalists tried the defences. The citizens heard a continuous rattle of muskets augmented by cannon fire. The worst menace came from the enemy trenches at Gaudy Green.

"They are digging deeper and deeper," one captain reported. "The Forest miners, we think. They certainly know what to do. We have seen timber supports and planks being taken underground."

"I'll show you what to do," declared Captain Harcus.

"That's the way," Massey said approvingly as the two captains left Greyfriars.

"There's a brick built house," said the first captain, "adjoining the city wall by the Rikenel. We have knocked a low doorway out of it so you can cross the outer moat using a bridge of ladders. I'll come with you."

"No you won't," Harcus said. "At least not this time. I want you to see how it is done. More important, I want you and your men to give us covering fire."

"You shall have that," the captain promised.

The daylight sortie proved as successful as the night one. Harcus and his soldiers forced the workmen either to flee or be taken prisoner along with their implements. Royalist troops, trying to retaliate, were unable to do so by a veritable rain of fire. More digging implements were captured and the entire workings brought to a halt.

"But not for long," Massey commented when the Forest men were brought before him. "Why do you do this to us? The city has always purchased your coal and the weapons you forged."

The miners looked down and shuffled their feet.

"You are prisoners," the colonel went on. "We'll feed you in return for work. Captain, hand them over to Under Sheriff Hill, then you and your men may go off duty."

"And so should you, Edward," Pudsey suggested.

"Nonsense!" said Massey. "What's the next problem?"

"Problems you mean."

"Let's have them then. You're wasting time."

"The enemy are grouping at Kingsholm. Heavy cannon is also being brought to bear on the wall sector between East and Southgate. Similar emplacements are going up near Llanthony and across Gaudy Green."

"Let's start with Kingsholm. Who's on duty there?"

"Captin Gray."

"He must counter-attack with a sufficient number of musketeers and pikemen. Not too little or too many, you understand."

"About 150 I would guess."

"No guesswork, Henry. Let Gray make a local decision. As to the enemy cannon between East and Southgates, our walls there look weak. That is from the outside. However the earthworks and filled-in houses should hold."

"There are still weak spots," Pudsey said.

"Then more earth and stones are needed. Ever thicker and higher." Massey smiled without much mirth. "Leave the Llanthony and Gaudy Green emplacements for the time being. It's low ground there by the river. No place for an attack."

That afternoon Captain Gray and 150 men went out against the besiegers at Kingsholm. The fight was a bloody one. A Royalist captain and nine soldiers were killed, also five taken prisoner. Before the enemy could counter-attack, Gray managed to set fire to the Kingsholm houses. He lingered dangerously long beside the spreading blaze as his men made their way back into the city.

"Good man!" Massey commended Gray on his return.

"We did not suffer a single casualty."

"It is said that fortune favours the brave." The colonel suddenly turned and asked Pudsey, "What day is this?"

"Saturday. You're dropping on your feet, sir."

"Saturday is it? The twelfth of August? Then both of us have been up for some time. We are being stupid. One must sleep while the other watches. So Henry, you go first."

"This is where I disobey you, Edward. You have had the heaviest burdens on your shoulders. Therefore you should go first."

"Shall we toss a coin?"

"That's gambling, sir. I don't feel tired now, but you look extremely tired. Please go and have some rest."

"On one condition, Henry. You are to wake me if anything untoward happens."

"You have my promise on that."

"Right." Edward Massey's shoulders visibly sagged.

At headquarters, two officers lay dozing in chairs and Thomas Hobart was curled up beside the door. Massey remarked to Pudsey,

"The sound sleep of the young, eh Henry."

"Try to emulate Tom." The sergeant major took a firm hold of his commander and propelled him to an inner room. No sooner had Pudsey shut the door than a lieutenant came from Captain Crispe in charge of the river sector. He said,

"I have to speak to the colonel."

"He is resting. You will speak with me. Quietly."

"You know the boat bridge we partly destroyed? More craft are being brought down from Tewkesbury."

That Sunday morning in Gloucester was strangely quiet. A heavy mist, like a harbinger of the coming autumn, lay with the enemy round the city. When it lifted, the watchers on the walls saw the same scene as before. Camp lines and outposts covered the countryside.

While the last shreds of mist were evaporating, Colonel Massey made his way along the walls. He kept warning officers and men not to relax their guard because it was Sunday. Despite his repeated warnings, the Puritan preachers of Gloucester were equally adamant about holding full length services. As one said,

"At such times, we should speak God's words."

"But not for three hours," Massey retorted.

The preacher frowned. He had his hour glass with him. On Sunday mornings, it was turned over again and again.

Fortunately the morning remained quiet. There was little activity around the Royalist camp. In the city, housewives supplied meals — cooked before the Sabbath — to the men on duty. Massey ate his at Greyfriars headquarters, talking to the young runners.

"When you have finished, I want you to inform all duty captains of the following two orders. First, they are to discourage sightseers. I personally had to turn away a family with little children strolling about the walls. Secondly, officers and men must maintain a constant watch on the enemy. If the enemy suspects an unguarded viewpoint, he will probe and enter. I know I would."

Thomas had been allocated the south eastern sector. Starting at the old castle, he went from officer to officer, always taking care to keep his head down. At one emplacement, he met Captain Alan Pury who jokingly asked,

"Where's your pony, Tom?"

"In the stables, sir."

"Oh, we thought you'd come round on it." Pury remarked and the men about him laughed.

Further laughter ended in a horrible gurgling sound, followed by a dull thud.

"Stay here, Tom," Pury ordered as he went to investigate.

"What happened, sir?" Thomas enquired when the captain returned.

"One of my men stood up to look over the wall. He's taken a bullet in his throat."

By now, musket shots were being exchanged along the line. The sharp cracks increased until they were non-stop. After a time, Pury said,

"You can continue, Tom, but keep below the wall."

"What of the soldier, sir."

"Dead, Tom. His lungs filled with blood."

The uneasy Sunday continued. Colonel Massey held a conference with his captains then reported to the committee of defence which had met in emergency session. Massey said,

"We have countered everything the enemy has so far attempted. I have no doubt they will continue their efforts as we shall ours. The main threat lies at Kingsholm."

"I understood," said Mayor Wise, "you'd burnt out that nest?"

"Temporarily. However the Royalists are moving more cannon there. We must make another sortie."

"Today?" Alderman Pury queried.

"Why yes, in an hour's time. Captain Mallery and 150 men have already been briefed and are standing by."

"Could it not wait until tomorrow? The preachers are complaining about violations of the Sabbath. Even this meeting is frowned upon."

"We must strike while the iron's hot."

"What about after midnight?"

"Too obvious."

"Well," Pury sighed, "I leave it to you, colonel. We may not consider such niceties later on, but on this first Sunday of the siege, I submit it is a delicate matter. The Puritans may appeal direct to the rank and file."

"To disobey my orders, sir?"

"I leave it to you," Alderman Pury repeated.

Against his better judgement, Massey delayed the sortie until first light on the Monday morning. The enemy were alert and a sharp skirmish took place. Captain Mallery reported back that he was fortunate to suffer no casualties.

"I hope the enemy did," Colonel Massey retorted.

"Four dead, sir, and two prisoners."

"Hand them over to Under Sheriff Hill and mention they may have information."

Soon after this incident, Thomas Hobart came running with a message from Captain Pury.

"Sir, he says the fire from the Royalist cannon at his sector is becoming effective. Part of the outer wall has fallen down."

Massey was out of the room in a flash. He found the breach was not as big as he feared and could be repaired by earth and stones. What concerned Massey more, were the trenches dipping into tunnels across Gaudy Green. The Royalist sappers had worked on them throughout Sunday.

"Why," he whirled on Alan Pury, "weren't they attacked?"

"The sappers were heavily guarded, sir."

"You'll rectify your inaction," Massey glared at the alderman's son. "Now!"

"Sergeant!" Captain Pury shouted. "I want one hundred men for an immediate sortie."

The raiders went out and were instantly pinned down by heavy Royalist fire. It took two hours of retaliatory fire from the city to retrieve them with the loss of five men. As Colonel Massey waited on the battlements, scowling in frustration, he suddenly noticed that the moat was lower. Somehow the enemy had managed to drain it.

Faith Merrett was hanging up washing in the back garden when a shadow fell across her. Turning she saw her father looking old and tired.

"Father!" Faith exclaimed. "How good to see you here."

"I was passing."

"I am glad you did not pass by. Would you care to come inside?"

"No Faith, the sun out here is kind to my old bones."

"Then sit on the bench beside the wall."

Alderman Pury sat for some time taking in the scene. Faith had done much with the back yard. A creeper hid most of Nathan's workshop, while the cows and chickens were kept at the far end. There a line of trees made cool greens between red brick buildings. Above everything, stone white in the summer sky, soared the tower of Gloucester cathedral.

"Of late," Pury said at last, "I have become too caught up in our city troubles. One still has family commitments."

"Dear father." Faith kissed him tenderly.

"Let us talk about our family then," Pury smiled. "Your mother is well, despite being an invalid these last twenty years. I envy her ability to ignore all that is going on around her. Even the wounded in her house she left to you."

"I was pleased to help."

"You did and now they've gone elsewhere."

"How is Alan?"

"Still impetuous, but I am sure Colonel Massey has the measure of him. An incredible man Massey. We are fortunate in having him at this time. He is straightforward, he is fair and he seems able to overcome every tribulation. If we fail, it will not be his fault."

"Will we fail, father?" Faith lowered her voice.

"Only the Lord knows. At least the Royalists are acting as Massey predicted. They keep pushing and so do we. The colonel believes we can remain on top until relief arrives."

"Any word of that?"

"None. But I came here to get away from such matters. How is Nathan? He seems busy and contented with the tasks Massey sets him."

"Yes, I believe he is."

"Have you some cool milk?" Faith's father asked.

"Certainly." She went to get it and, on her return, found him dozing. Pury slept for several minutes before jerkng awake.

"What . . .?" he gazed blankly around him. "I am an old man indeed."

"You're overworked. Here is the milk you wanted."

"The cows seem to keep on producing." Pury looked in the direction of Mary and Martha. "You are a good housekeeper Faith, and much missed in my home. What other news have I for you? Ah yes! You remember that lieutenant you nursed twice? Richard Gwinnett?"

"Yes father."

"He went to see Colonel Massey a few days ago and offered his services. Massey pointed out that a soldier without a right arm could not really help him. To this Gwinnett replied, 'I do not mind what is required of me, so long as I can continue to serve the Parliamentary cause.' "

"It has served him ill," Faith remarked.

"Mm," her father nodded. "The colonel then had a good idea. He is clever that Massey. Present him with any problem and he sets about solving it. As you know Tobias Jordan has been unwell — or claims he is — so John Dorney is more often than not at Greyfriars with the colonel. To cut a long story short, Massey sent Gwinnett to me."

"To you?"

"At first I was perplexed about what to do with him, but the lieutenant has proved useful. To start with he is well read, also has taught himself to write with his left hand. Not too well as yet, but it is a start. The main point is Richard Gwinnett's helping me a great deal."

"I am glad to hear that, father. You need all the help you can get."

"He does so without interfering or, more important, without upsetting other members of the committee. Yes, Gwinnett has proved himself in many ways. He keeps me in touch with John Dorney. He helps to organise the gunpowder factories. He has simplified the lists and whereabouts of billeted soldiers. He even sees your husband on carpentry requirements."

"Nathan says he likes to help where he can. Besides we need the money. Have you any more interesting news, father?"

"Only that Richard Gwinnett has a constant visitor in young Thomas Hobart. Whenever Tom has a spare moment, he never fails to call on Richard."

"The lad misses his father and Nathan has never filled the gap."

"You're full of commonsense."

"Which I learned from you."

"Our talk has done me a power of good." Alderman Pury rose. While doing so, the smile on his face faded. "One can hardly believe — standing here in your garden — we are besieged and in mortal peril."

"Dear father." Faith embraced him. She appreciated only too well that King Charles knew Pury and would put the whole responsibility of Gloucester's resistance on those frail shoulders. An alderman, though high in the city, was of low rank to a king. Such subjects were not favoured with the swift extinction of the axe. Faith shuddered at the thought.

"What is the matter, my dear?"

"Nothing. I am just sad at your departure." She walked with him to the front of the house. "Come again, father. Come every day if you are able. Since I left home, I have not had such a pleasant conversation."

"While I," Pury said sadly, "do not enjoy the same in my own house. What ridiculous lives we lead, Faith. Planning, scheming, accumulating wealth and position — all for what?"

With this thought, Alderman Pury set off down Westgate Street shaking his venerable head.

The partial draining of the moat was not so disastrous as Massey had feared. The moat only ran outside the oldest part of the city wall and, half drained, revealed a deep ditch which any enemy would find hard to cross. Moreover, Colonel Massey noted, the water had seeped into the Royalist trenches and mines, thereby rendering them useless.

Notwithstanding, the enemy had commenced another trench and mine system. Forest of Dean men, whom the Gloucester citizens likened to moles, were busy digging themselves down into the earth. The efforts of these lowly miners were encouraged by the Royalist nobility.

"Prince Rupert is always there," Pudsey observed.

"Everything to do with war interests him," replied Massey. "He learns all the time. That is why he is such a formidable opponent." The colonel screwed up his eyes then said, "I do believe we could reach those mineheads by grenade throwing. That is, if there are any good throwers in Gloucester."

That afternoon, Captain Harcus who had done such valiant work from

Northgate, came to watch the grenade throwing. The grenades were effective but few reached the distance. Impatiently, Harcus took a grenade and hurled it. He then stood to watch. As the grenade reached its target, Harcus fell with musket shots through his chest.

Massey was resting when the news was brought to him.

"With your permission sir," said Captain Pury, "We wish to take a force of 200 men and destroy that minehead. If the enemy interferes, so much the worse for them."

"Harcus was my friend," Captain Crispe added. "I wish to accompany Captain Pury. So do Harcus's men."

"Such raids," said Massey, "as best accomplished in the heat of the moment. I shall cover you with cannon fire. If you get into trouble, we shall join you."

"It is the enemy who will be in trouble," Crispe informed him, "judging from the mood of my men."

The strong vengeful party marched under the walls to Friars Orchard and straight away fell on the enemy trenches. Boards were torn up, grenades were thrown and the muddy miners either shot or cut down. All the while, Massey poured shot overhead to keep back the main Royalist force.

To his surprise, Captains Pury and Crispe, with their 200 strong raiding party still intact, did not immediately return after wrecking the mine. Instead they headed for a large group of Royalists. Massey had to cease firing so as not to hit any of his own men.

A confused hand-to-hand fight took place. The defenders on the walls could hear men shouting and see them falling. They could also observe the rest of the Royalist camp. At first there was a ripple of confusion, then more and more enemy soldiers began hurrying towards the trouble spot.

"Break off!" Massey called. "Break off and return."

To his relief, he saw Alan Pury look back then give orders. The Parliamentary party was able to disengage just in time. They came towards the walls, with several of their comrades being helped by others. The moment the last man was within the required distance, Massey ordered covering fire to re-commence over them.

"We killed dozens," Crispe reported later, "with only a few wounded on our side. I would say that Captain Harcus has been revenged."

It was a triumph though only a small one. No sooner had the raiding party disappeared than Prince Rupert came galloping towards the scene. Massey watched the prince assessing the extent of the damage and issuing fresh orders. Ignoring the mud and blood around him, and despite being impeccably dressed as usual, Rupert waded first into the approach trench, then entered the devastated mine.

Within an hour, hundreds more Forest of Dean miners were on the way. Carts brought new timber supports and planks. Cannon were shifted to cover every approach to the mine workings. Two troops of dragoons were positioned on either side. Massey remarked to Pudsey,

"He has done what I would have done. Now I am going to do what he may think I dare not. We raid tonight. As soon as it is dark enough. In strength."

Massey led the raid himself. He picked his men, armed them only with pistols and swords, ordered them to wear dark clothes and blacken their faces. Within seconds of their slipping through the gates, the night swallowed them up.

More seconds passed. All of a sudden there were shouts and flashes. Thomas Hobart, who was on the wall, saw torches being lit in the Royalist camp. Occasionally he caught glimpses of men fighting, but the incident seemed to be made up of flashing lights, moving in aimless patterns.

Ten minutes later, the raiding party was back inside the city walls. It was well over an hour before the Royalist camp settled down, then Massey hit them again. This time, he took another party of fresh men to strike at the same target.

This second raid roused the Royalist camp for several hours. Eventually they grew quiet, only to be stirred once more by a third sortie launched just before the dawn.

"Well Henry," Colonel Massey declared, when he was back in Greyfriars, shedding ripped and powder stained clothes, "we have taught them not one lesson but three."

"You have, Edward."

"If you were the enemy," Massey asked, while putting on a fresh shirt and tucking it into his breeches, "what would you do next?"

"Rupert has been concentrating his cannon. I believe he will send shot over our walls and into the city. We are in for a heavy pounding."

From that day onwards — Thursday 17th August — great numbers of cannon balls began to fall on Gloucester. By some strange freak the majority landed in streets and did no harm. Four however hit houses. They went through rooves, ceilings and floors as if each was made of paper.

One cannon ball started a fire and, here again, only pure chance prevented the house being burned down. A woman happened to be passing with a pail of water and threw it over the first flickering flames. After the ball had cooled, the occupants of the house weighed it. The weight was sixty pounds.

When night followed that uneasy day, the Royalists sent parties of foot soldiers to test the defences. This also stopped attacks being made by the defenders. One large enemy force brought bundles of twigs to fill and cross the half drained moat. As with all the other raiders, this force was beaten off.

Yet one man got through. While most of the action seemed to be taking place along the north, east and south sides of the city, this man was ferried across the Severn and, on landing, he made for the town hall. There the man waited, crouched beside the front steps, until Richard Gwinnett arrived to open up in the morning.

"Who are you?" Gwinnett wanted to know. The man had a strange apprearance. He was dressed in good clothes yet looked a vagabond.

"I am from the King," said the man, "and I have papers for Alderman Pury."

There were soldiers passing at the time and Gwinnett called to them. He ordered,

"Guard this man while I get the alderman."

His intention proved easier said then done. Pury was in bed and slow to dress. He also insisted that Gwinnett fetch the rest of the committee saying he would not open any message from the King without the others being present.

"Colonel Massey should be there," Pury told Gwinnett, while his swollen fingers grappled with belts and thongs. "And what about Tobias Jordan?" His mysterious illness has gone on far too long."

In the end, the entire committee, with Massey and Jordan included, assembled. Only then did Pury send for the messenger.

"Your name?"

"Jack Barstow."

"Occupation?"

"Oh, this and that."

"Do not trifle with us," Pury warned.

"I used to work in the King's stables. Wherever he held his court. Later I was used as a messenger. The King never saw me, you understand. Others brought me messages and gave me instructions about delivering them."

"How did you get into Gloucester?" Massey wanted to know.

"By boat."

"The papers," Alderman Pury was now impatient to see them.

There were two papers. One was a broadsheet, the other a personal letter.

"Open the broadsheet first," Pury instructed.

The sheet had been printed at Oxford and comprised three pieces of text separated by ruled lines. The first two were preproductions of the King's original offer to Gloucester and the city's reply. The third text read,

"Let the world now judge if his Majesty could have sent a more gracious message to his most loyal subjects and whether these desperate rebels deserve any mercy.

"After so many offers they still refuse our pardon and even when returning their rebellious answer did set fire to their own suburbs which surely is not to keep the city for King and Parliament."

"I presume this broadsheet," Mayor Wise addressed the messenger, "is being nailed up the length and breath of England?"

"It has also been sent abroad," Barstow informed him.

"No doubt."

"His Majesty," Alderman Pury nodded, "has merely made a debating point about us firing the suburbs."

"It was a military necessity," Colonel Massey declared.

"No one is disputing that," Pury said. "As to the personal letter, Richard Gwinnett should open and read it to us, after which we can discuss same." Acting on these instructions, Richard read,

"We knew you and your family in better days and it is still our belief that those more pleasant times can return to our mutual advantage.

"We have the whole country save Gloucester and London and would be magnanimous to both should you set the example and return to the friendship you once showed.

"You would find us generous to you personally and merciful to all who were so misguided as to oppose us.

"What we propose is that you leave Gloucester in our safekeeping and go to London to convince your friends there of our intention to unite the nation under our beneficent rule."

"Well?" asked Pury when Gwinnett had stopped reading.

"Well, there are no threats with this message," Mayor Wise remarked.

"I think we should respond," Tobias Jordan said eagerly. "The King has come to his senses. We must take advantage of it."

Jordan's suggestion was drowned by the rest of the committee,

"The King has never kept his word."

"To anyone."

"There are no guarantees."

"If we surrender, he would not allow one of us to live."

"After all our efforts . . ."

"Yes gentlemen!" Colonel Massey stood up and hammered his clenched fist on the table. "After all our efforts. After Captain Harcus and other good men have died for us. After our three raids in one night. After your citizens have unceasingly carried baskets of earth and stone. What would they say if their leaders gave in now?"

"Many sir," Tobias Jordan stood up facing the colonel, "are not in favour of this war. We Puritans are not men of blood like you."

"Let us," Alderman Pury sighed, "put the matter to vote."

By a majority decision, it was decided to continue with the siege. Councillor Jordan and two of his friends asked that their dissenting votes be placed on record.

"To cover yourselves," Massey sneered.

The committee of defence then decided not to return any message to the King. Jack Barstow was simply given a safe passage and bundled out of the city.

After he had gone, the councillors turned to other matters. When the meeting came to 'any other business', Pury asked Jordan,

"Are you now back with us, Tobias?"

"I am still poorly . . ."

"So are my men in the common grave," Massey commented.

"Please colonel," Pury murmured. He then addressed Jordan in a voice of silk. "You have absented yourself for some time. You have this morning spoken of giving in to the King. It would seem that you are not for Gloucester."

"The city has always had my best interests," Jordan answered. "We differ on the right course to take at this moment."

"At this moment therefore," Pury's voice became quieter still, "are you with us or against us? Do you wish to remain a member of this committee?

"Er, yes . . ."

"What does that mean?"

"You must forgive me," Lawyer Jordan looked round the table. "I have not been well."

"Speaking for myself," said Alderman Pury, "I have been put to a great deal of inconvenience by not having John Dorney here, though Richard Gwinnett has been most useful. All this Tobias, was due to your absence. I expect you to return to Greyfriars."

"The present arrangements are working well enough" said Massey but Pury was adamant.

"You will have Councillor Jordan, colonel and try to imbue him with some of your military fire. As for you Richard, you can help John though be aware, I have other plans for you. We are entering a new and vital stage of the siege. If events favour us, you will be very busy — very busy indeed."

Alderman Pury was right. A fresh phase had begun in the siege of Gloucester. Mining activities were temporarily halted while the Royalist artillery came forward to show the King what could be accomplished. The batteries on the south side of the city did little harm, due to the thickness of walls supplemented by inner earthworks. However a new battery of cannon, firing from Kingsholm, sorely tried the northern sector.

"It cannot be allowed to continue," Colonel Massey said to his captains. "All guns at Kingsholm must be spiked."

"They are being protected by strong enemy forces," said Captain Gray, whose sector it was, and Captain Faulkner, who shared the duty with him, agreed.

"Then we must have a stronger force," Massey argued.

"It would have to be upwards of 300 men."

"Very well, 400."

"With me leading it," Sergeant Major Pudsey volunteered. "We'll need several officers to manage such a force, also a diversion in another direction."

The plan was put into immediate effect. A diversionary force of 50 musketeers, led by Lieutenant Pincocke, pretended to be making for the village of Sandhurst. No sooner had the enemy started towards them, than Pudsey led out his 400 men at the double. The Royalist cannon posed no danger, being at elevated positions for bombarding the city. Before the gunners could lower muzzles, Pudsey's men were in among them. Pincocke also turned and led in his smaller party.

During the slaughter of over 100 Royalist officers and men, Sergeant Major Pudsey calmly spiked every gun. Working slowly and professionally, he appeared oblivious of the hand to hand fighting going on around him.

By way of retaliation, Royalist artillery on the other side of Gloucester began a devastating bombardment. Colonel Massey hastily crossed the city to see what was happening and found Alderman Pury on the wall by the Rikenel

"Sir," said Massey, "you should not be endangering yourself."

"One place is as safe as another," Pury replied. "I have counted 150 cannonballs aimed at this sector alone. Can the wall withstand such a fierce bombardment?"

"If not the wall," Massey explained, "the earthworks will. They are our greatest protection, absorbing the shot. I have witnessed the effect several times in the Low Countries."

Massey was amused to see Tobias Jordan crouching round a corner, well out of danger. He was about to remark on it when cheering rose from the street. A crowd had gathered round a dead pig killed by an almost spent cannonball bouncing along the ground.

"Can we roast and eat it?" a citizen asked Alderman Pury.

"I have no objection. What do you think, colonel?"

"On one condition," Massey said, "you let the Royalists know first. They may think we are starving in here. But be careful. Raise the roasted carcase on pike points. Do not show yourselves."

Alderman Pury did not say anything as they walked back to Greyfriars. Outside the colonel's headquarters however, he stopped and said,

"Our pig will be famous."

"Yes," Massey agreed," and it has served to put our men in high spirits. There is nothing better for morale than an unexpected feast. No doubt the tale will be told and retold for generations.

"That is what I mean. Tobias," Pury turned to Jordan who had grown calmer with every step away from the fighting. "You are fortunate in being a witness to such an incident. One can learn much from common pleasures. With courage so high under our military commander, I doubt the King can defeat us."

But the King's artillery thought otherwise. The incident of the pig, whose roasted carcase was carried jeeringly along the wall, caused the guns to fire all the more. Cannonballs of every size showered on the city throughout the day and into the night.

A fifty pounder hit the top of a house and smashed through the roof. Another fell floor by floor until it landed in the kitchen between three women sitting by the fire. Others rolled casually along streets and a boy who tried to halt one lost his foot.

Instinctively Colonel Massey felt that a Royalist attack would be launched. He ordered the watches on the walls to be doubled and drums sounded throughout the night to keep everyone on the alert.

Shortly after midnight, shouts from the Rikenel area told of a Royalist assault where the moat was half drained and the wall damaged. Troops pounding along the street wakened Thomas Hobart lying in Greyfriars.

For the first time he could remember, the room was empty. Three candles had been burning. Some harnesses swung by the open door. There was more running outside and hoarse shouts.

"The Rikenel!"

"Heavy attack."

Slipping on his shoes, Thomas ventured on to the now deserted street. Ahead he could hear the sound of muskets. A soldier came reeling past him, coughed and fell down. Two more soldiers carrying several carbines apiece shoved Tom to one side. Ahead were the earthworks silhouetted against a glowing sky.

Waves of soldiers were rushing up the earthworks and descending the far slope. Tom went to the top and found himself looking into what he imagined when Puritan preachers talked about the horrors of The Pit.

Below him in the muddy moat, partly bridged by bundles of sticks and chunks of fallen wall, men swarmed like soldier ants in their attempts to slaughter each other. Many had succeeded and the rest were trampling their victims into the morass in order to survive themselves.

Thomas saw the effects of carbines being fired at close quarters, of heavy muskets being used as bone-smashing clubs and the dreaded swords swung by experts. Bloody pieces of human beings flew through the air. The shouts and shrieks were unearthly. Every few seconds more men would drop into the pit, landing on friend and foe alike; slipping, slithering on each other as they killed or were killed.

Vomit rose from Tom's stomach, leaving him dangerously weak. He tottered by the edge of the pit. Fortunately a hand caught him by the collar. His rescuer was Richard Gwinnett.

"Come," the lieutenant said, "you should not be here."

Gwinnett took him home. The front door of the Merrett's house was wide open due to the soldiers billeted there having left in a hurry. When Gwinnett entered the hallway, Faith called from the stairs,

"Who's there? What is happening?"

"I have brought Tom home," the lieutenant replied.

"Has anything happened to him?"

"No, he's all right, but have you a light?"

The hallway and stairwell were in darkness until Nathan Merrett appeared with a candle. While Faith attended to Tom, Nathan and Richard sat wearily in the kitchen. The Puritan asked,

"Have they broken through?"

"No," Gwinnett said again, "though it has been a bloody business. Unfortunately Tom saw it."

At that moment Faith joined them, drawing a cloak round her.

"Let us pray," she said, "he doesn't have nightmares."

"Let us all pray." Nathan took their hands.

The Royalist attack was beaten off and, during the following day, thanksgiving services were held in the city. These services were combined with funeral ones because no fewer than sixteen officers and men had died in repulsing the enemy, while three times that number were grieveously wounded. As he sat listening to the psalms and prayers, Colonel Massey hoped there would not be more such serious assaults.

Meanwhile Sergeant Major Pudsey toured the defences to make sure everyone was on the alert. Nothing missed his experienced eye, yet he made an error of judgement. The city battery near Westgate was headed by Master Gunner Hatton, who had installed and fired the city's first cannon. This battery was aimed across the river at the Welsh forces.

"Any sign of activity?" Pudsey asked.

"None sir." The gunner seemed strangely agitated, his eyebrows going up and down.

"Well, everything seems spick and span here." Pudsey looked around him. Hatton, he knew, was a professional, but what was the matter with the man?

"Who's horse is that?" The sergeant major glanced at a chestnut mare tethered nearby.

"One of the officers, sir. They take it in turns to have their horses graze on the rich grass down here."

"Mm, fine animal." Sergeant Major Pudsey left the gun emplacement and went towards the bridge. On reaching it, he asked about the horse and the duty officer stared at him. "That horse!" Pudsey pointed backwards without looking. "The chestnut mare." The officer stared all the more.

Turning, Pudsey saw the the horse had disappeared. For one moment, it seemed an impossibility, then he saw a horse's head in the river. Already the chestnut mare was close to the other side and steering it was Master Gunner Hatton. Pudsey could still see the agitated eyebrows.

There were shouts from the Welsh who ran from their lines to Hatton and the horse. Shooting broke out until the gunner was beyond range. Striding back to the emplacement, Pudsey indignantly questioned the gunnery assistants. They denied all knowledge of Hatton's intentions and, in the end, Pudsey was inclined to believe them.

"It is," he reported later to Massey, "our first desertion."

"I had expected it before now."

"But a master gunner?"

"He'll be welcome in the Royalist ranks."

"You are taking this lightly, Edward," Pudsey said. "The city has paid Hatton, also housed him comfortably for some time. Before you and I came here. Where's his loyalty?"

"Now that's a word." Colonel Massey gave a wry smile. "I'm only here because the King's army denied me preference. What about you, Henry? Be truthful."

"I am and always shall be a Parliamentarian," said the sergeant major. "This is our chance — the first in our history — to fight for the rights of honest, hard-working Englishmen. It's a matter of principle."

"Which is another word." Massey seemed in a flippant mood, yet what he said next was chilling. "By the way, if you capture Hatton, have him hanged at once."

The Royalist grip on the city tightened. During Monday 21st August, Colonel Massey sent out two strong raiding parties against guns hammering at Eastgate and Southgate. Both were repulsed before they could reach their objectives, the King's dragoons swooping on them. Casualties were high for both sides with Gloucester being least able to afford such losses.

"Not a good day," Massey later said to Pudsey.

"Decidedly not."

"Henry, do you feel we are beginning to lose?"

"Those are strange words coming from you, Edward."

"I am, as you know, a realist. Between ourselves, we cannot keep up this pace and we have no idea if Essex has received word from Gloucester, let alone is on his way to relieve us. I feel it has become a matter for more messengers."

"Will you first clear it with the committee of defence?"

"As usual Henry, you have gone to the heart of the matter. I do not want them to know the strength — or rather the weakness — of my feelings. Morale is still high among the men and in the city. We must keep it so."

"On the other hand, Pury would resent you communicating with Essex behind his back."

"I was thinking of communicating with my old friend Waller."

"He is a spent force and out of favour I'll warrant."

"But Waller would understand and he knows the right people. If the city messengers did arrive, all to the good. If they did not, then Waller would help."

"Who do you have in mind?"

"Sergeants Oakley and Summers."

"I see you've thought this out. Ex-sergeants of Waller."

"Yes, and good soldiers. If any two men can make it, they will. I want you to inform them Henry, swear them to secrecy, give them two horses apiece and have them here at midnight."

"How are you going to get them out of the city?"

"I have already arranged it. Midnight."

As the clocks of Gloucester struck twelve, Pudsey left the two sergeants with four horses outside Greyfriars and entered to fetch Massey.

"Are they there?" the colonel asked.

"Yes."

"Have they been briefed?"

"Of course."

"Then we are on our way. You have one of the spare horses while I lead with the other."

Massey took them through alleys that Pudsey never knew existed. It was so dark between the buildings that the sergeant major had no idea where they were until he heard the lapping of water.

"Are we at the docks?" he whispered to Massey.

"Ssh!"

A dark figure seemed to rise out of the ground, causing Pudsey to jump.

"This is Toby," Massey continued to whisper. "Someone who does special jobs for me. Toby is going to take the two sergeants and their horses. Has your craft been properly padded, Toby?"

"Aye sir. Handle the horses gently and no one will hear anything."

"Good. We'll put the horses aboard, then I'll have a last word with the sergeants."

The first horse was reluctant but the others followed easily. They were farm animals commandeered for war duties. Instinctively they knew there was no room for temperament in their new environment. The horses settled themselves in the bottom of the boat and remained still.

"Sergeants Oakley and Summers," Massey placed his arms round the soldiers shoulders and drew their heads together. "You have a secret mission and a great responsibility. We asked Parliament for help, but have heard nothing. Perhaps relief is on its way, yet we cannot rely on that. I am depending on you to reach your old commander and to tell him of our situation here.

"You have spare horses for the hundred mile ride and sufficient rations. Whether you go together or split up will be your decision. You are experienced soldiers. I need hardly tell you to avoid Oxford. You may care to go north or south of it. Or both. Again up to you.

"There is only one way I can personally help you." Massey placed a purse in each sergeant's hand. "Have a few drinks on me, but don't tell the preachers. Above all, keep out of trouble. Off you go. Toby will land you two miles downstream of the enemy. Circle round and head east. You should be on the high Cotswolds by dawn."

Gruffly the two sergeants thanked Massey and assured him they would do their best. A moment later they were in the boat attending to their horses. Toby immediately cast off and the craft began to drift downstream. Another moment and it had disappeared in the darkness.

"It is," Massey remarked to Pudsey, "as if nothing has occurred here."

"Apart from the muster rolls being short of two sergeants and four horses," Pudsey retorted.

"It takes a really clever sergeant major," said Massey, "to make the necessary adjustments. The main point is that two good men are on their way. I'll sleep easier tonight because of them."

"And I'll lie awake worrying," Pudsey said. "Worrying about altering those muster rolls."

When morning came, an uneasy silence lay over the city. The defenders were not wakened to cannon or musket fire. Instead those on watch saw the Royalists having their morning meal, parading and generally moving about the surrounding encampments. These innocuous activities continued until noon.

"What are they up to?" asked Pudsey. He was with Massey on their routine tour of the defences.

"His Royal Highness," Colonel Massey frowned, "is up to something."

"Sir," Tom came hurrying towards them, "Northgate reports that two men have come through the Royalist lines and asked permission to enter Gloucester."

"Two?" Massey, who thought of the sergeants, shot a glance at Pudsey.

"They're lawyers I believe, sir," Tom piped up.

"We'd better go and see," said Massey relieved.

The guardroom at Northgate was an untidy place with off duty soldiers sleeping where they could, those on standby eating and the accoutrements of war piled everywhere. In the centre of these seemingly haphazard activities stood two tall, grave, soberly dressed strangers. Colonel Massey introduced himself, then asked them who they were.

"I sir," the older man spoke in an unctuous voice, "am Mr. Bell from Sandhurst. And this sir, is Mr. Hill from Tewkesbury. We are lawyers, colleagues of Councillor Jordan and well known to Alderman Pury."

"And the purpose of your visit?" Massey asked sharply.

"Peace, sir." Mr. Bell glanced distastefully round the guardroom.

"The King's provost," said Mr. Hill, in a low sibilant voice, "who happens to be a legal acquaintance of ours, approached us yesterday. His Majesty is concerned by the loss of lives on both sides and has asked us to negotiate with your committee of defence."

"Papers!" the military governor snapped. "Your identifications. Safe passes."

He was playing for time but, as usual, lawyers had all the time in the world. Of course they had papers. More papers than Massey cared to peruse. In the end he had to say,

"Very well, if you'll accompany me, gentlemen."

Colonel Massey took them to The Cross, then briskly down Westgate. The lawyers' eyes, he noted, were everywhere.

"Has the city sustained much damage?" Mr. Bell enquired.

"Nothing much. A few roof tiles I believe."

"But the terrible shelling. People must have been killed."

"Our only casualty has been a pig and we roasted that." Massey increased his stride.

"I should imagine," came the sibilant, wheedling voice of Mr. Hill, 'that life here has become most difficult. What with the lack of food, water supplies and normal commerce."

"We have food stocks for over two years," Massey retorted, "and, as for water, it flows past us. You know Gloucester. One only has to dig a hole and there it is. We would willingly give half of our water away."

"Yes, but commerce," Hill persisted. "everything has to be paid for. You cannot continue — the way you're doing — indefinitely. Reason must prevail."

"I am but a soldier, sir," said Massey. "You'd better argue that with the committee."

At the town hall, Colonel Massey left the two lawyers with John Dorney and Richard Gwinnett, then went to Alderman Pury's office.

"I know Bell," said Pury when Massey had explained the situation. "A trimmer if ever there was one. And I've heard of Hill. Tobias Jordan is friendly with both of them. They'll no doubt want to see me and Tobias, but it must be the full committee of defence. Is Jordan at Greyfriars?"

"He should be."

"Tell Gwinnett to fetch him and all the other members. Those lawyers are to remain with John Dorney until we are in session. Can you spare time from your military duties, colonel and join us?"

"Everything is quiet at the moment."

"Well, hand over to Pudsey and be here."

Eventually the two lawyers were brought into the chamber and introduced to everyone present. They were given comfortable chairs and, as Massey noted, Alderman Pury adopted an air of affability.

"I hope you are both at ease, gentlemen? Any refreshments or services you may require are available to you. We pride ourselves in Gloucester for our courtesy and hospitality."

"You are very relaxed, sir," Mr. Bell began, "considering the seriousness of your situation."

"When one has right on one's side," Pury answered, "one's conscience rests easily. But please, you are here to discuss the situation. Pray do so."

"Mr. Hill and I," Bell said, "were approached yesterday by Mr. Abercombie, His Majesty's legal adviser. Mr. Abercombie told us how sad the King was at the continued resistance of Gloucester. He has a profound affection for this city and therefore no wish for it to be treated like Bristol. Through Mr. Abercombie, His Majesty reaffirmed he would welcome any endeavour to reach a reasonable solution."

"There now," said Councillor Jordan looking to either side of him. The rest of the committee stared solidly ahead.

"Specifically," said Pury, "what sort of solution?"

"May I interrupt here," Mayor Wise leaned forward. "The history of this reign has been made up of the King proposing solutions and his creatures acting otherwise."

"Ahem," Mr. Hill's thin voice entered the conversation. "Could we keep our discussion in sequence? Legal training y'know, eh Tobias?"

"Yes, yes," said Jordan.

"After long and detailed discussions with Mr. Abercombie," Bell went on, "His Majesty graciously invited us to dine with him. At Matson House. There we met his military secretary, Sir Jacob Ashley, Lords Ruthen and Chandos, Princess Rupert and Maurice, also young Prince Charles and the Duke of York."

"A splendid evening," Mr. Hill confirmed.

"Which reminds me," said Alderman Pury. "I hope that you gentlemen will be joining us for a more humble repast. Please excuse me one moment while I arrange it."

Colonel Massey and the committee members were somewhat perplexed when Pury left the chamber. Their austere leader did not normally concern himself with mere food. In fact Pury was the most abstemious of men and seldom noticed what he was eating.

Outside Alderman Pury hurried up to Gwinnett and said,

"Richard, I want you to perform an important task for me. It may not seem so, but you must do exactly what I say. You know my daughter, Faith Merrett. You are to go directly to her with the following instructions . . ."

Back in the council chamber, Pury apologised for his interruption of the proceedings and begged the lawyers to tell of their conversation with King Charles.

"During dinner," Mr. Bell said, "His Majesty was charming to both of us. He stressed the invaluable work accomplished by country lawyers in maintaining the legal framework of his kingdom and he spoke of preferment — for subjects of like mind — as soon as this unfortunate conflict could be resolved.

"As to Gloucester, His Majesty was genuinely distressed. Here, he said, is a fine city situated at the crossroads of England, set to grow and to prosper, yet held back by resistance to just conditions accepted by the rest of the country."

"Apart from London and a few isolated places, the King rules and is made welcome. He hopes that Parliament will soon see sense and allow him to return to his capital.

"But it is Gloucester that is His Majesty's main concern. That is closest to his heart. It distresses him that your soldiers should die and your citizens suffer due to a mere difference of political opinion. Something which we lawyers could so easily sort out.

"I assure you gentlemen, His Majesty fully understands your cause. He is aware of your concern and he wishes to resolve the matter in the best possible way. To his mind and to ours, the best possible way is by a legal solution to which all men of good will should agree."

"What are," asked Alderman Pury, "his specific proposals?"

"They are short and simple." Mr. Hill took a sheet of paper from an inner pocket. "First, that you cease all resistance and open the gates of Gloucester. Second, that you lay down your arms to the King's appointed officers. Third, that you welcome your Sovereign into his city. Fourth, that you send word to Parliament to this effect. Fifth, that your soldiers either join His Majesty's forces or disperse after an oath never to take up arms against him. Sixth, that you accept the jurisdiction of the King's appointed governor and garrison in this city."

"We come now," Mr. Bell took over, "to His Majesty's promises. You will appreciate that he has to tread warily here because at present you are declared traitors. I assured him, whenever I could, that you were the most loyal of subjects and he graciously conceded such could be the case."

"The promises," Mayor Wise murmured. "Are they written down, signed and sealed, like the six proposals?"

"Not at the moment," Mr. Bell looked uncomfortable.

"Then may we hear them? From your mouth."

"Alderman Pury sir, in return for your travelling to London and convincing Parliament as to the righteousness of the King's cause, he would subsequently honour and enrich you. He promises the same for the rest of this committee. Puritans will be permitted the full practice of their religion provided that no more opposition is made to the King's own church."

"Well," said Pury, "we have six specific proposals and some hints of preferment. Speaking for myself, I am reluctant to travel to London, then try pleading the King's cause in Parliament. However, let us discuss the matter."

By one o'clock, it had become evident that the gap between what the King wanted and what Gloucester would accept remained impossibly wide.

"You must admit," Mr. Hill kept insisting, "you are in the weakest of positions. The King's army surrounds you. No help can reach you. The King commands the entire hundred miles between Gloucester and London. Why suffer and starve?"

"We neither suffer nor starve," Pury said indignantly. "Our humble tables cannot compare with those of the court, yet we manage to keep body and soul together. John, would you please have Richard bring in our meagre council fare."

The councillors' eyes widened when they saw the food and drink Faith had obtained from her father's household. There were liberal cuts of cold meat, a hot pie, breasts and legs of chicken, salads, bread rolls and fresh fruit. All were served on the Pury plate. The crowning glory of this meal was the superb selection of German and French wines from the alderman's cellar. Pury who seldom touched wine was now topping up the lawyer's goblets and proposing toast after toast. A party atmosphere began to develop.

This was dispelled when the discussions recommenced. Neither side made any headway and Pury summed up by saying,

"I am afraid that those are our unswerving views, gentlemen. Please convey them to the King. Tell him he has but to agree with Parliament and he would not find more loyal subjects than in Gloucester."

It was then that Mr. Hill drew a chill over the proceedings, his sibilant voice making the threat all the more menacing. He remarked,

"Last night at dinner, one of the noblemen — it was I believe Lord Chandos — described Gloucester. He mentioned there were twelve inns."

"Correct," Mayor Wise nodded.

"Later someone else mentioned there were twelve city councillors and this coincidence amused the King. In fact, His Majesty remarked . . ."

"As a jest I'm sure," Mr. Bell interrupted, but Hill would not be deflected,

"The King said that the twelve signs would be convenient to hang a same number of councillors."

There was a long silence broken at last by Pury murmuring,

"No one can say we did not have a frank exchange of views. Please sirs, convey our words to the King. Colonel Massey will return you to Northgate."

Less than an hour after the local lawyers had left the city, the Royalist bombardment recommenced. Coincidentally a large cannonball hit the Crown Inn, smashing its sign. Later rain fell heavily and the firing ceased.

During the night, after the rain clouds had passed over the Severn Valley, the watch reported a bonfire on top of Wainlode Hill. Massey was roused and he hurried to Northgate because, prior to the siege, a friend of John Dorney had promised to light such a fire if relief was near the city.

"What do you think?" Pudsey asked Massey.

"I would like to believe relief is close, but it is too good to be true."

"Why do you say so?"

"Mr. Bell lives at the foot of Wainlode. He may have heard of the arrangement."

As usual, Faith was the first to rise in the Merrett household. While dressing she gazed with affection at the familiar view down Westgate to the river. Despite the siege, the outlook was unchanged. Outside lay the same red roof tops, the same green meadows and the same dear river flowing down to the sea.

After dressing, Faith looked at the twins. They were asleep in each other's arms as usual, smiling to each other as always. Anne and Jane Merrett disturbed Faith though she never could quite understand why. At least they got on well with Mrs Curtis. The widow liked talking and the twins were content to listen.

Quietly Faith descended to the kitchen then went to milk Mary and Martha. She enjoyed milking them, especially on an August morning after the night's rain. Tom would be along soon for he had come off duty early in the evening.

"Hello Thomas," Faith greeted him. "Slept well?"

"Yes thank you."

"Are you on duty today?"

"From noon. I can take Mary and Martha to the near meadows. It is their turn."

"That would help me. I have much to do." They milked for a while in silence, then Faith enquired,

"Do you like working for Colonel Massey?"

"Yes," Tom said slowly, "he is quick and decisive . . ."

"But?"

"I'll never make a soldier." Thomas thought about this statement before continuing. "I strive to do my duty, yet my heart is not in it."

"Or in furniture making." Faith made a joke of this. "You are still young, Tom. Who knows what will happen to each of us when this war is over. We can only live for the day."

Faith took up her pail of milk and returned to the kitchen. There, to her surprise, she found Peggy red-eyed from a night's sobbing.

"Why Peg," Faith put down the pail and hugged her little maid. "Whatever is the matter with you?"

"My man," Peggy began to wail. "He has disappeared."

"Your man?"

Peggy sniffed a bit more before saying,

"I am not with child, if that's what you're thinking."

"Of course not." Faith was relieved. The Puritans could be hard on an unlucky girl.

"I love him," Peggy said, "and he loves me. He told me when this war is over, he wants to settle down here in Gloucester even though he comes from Devon."

"Well," Faith smiled, "I've learned he loves you and he comes from Devon. May I ask his name, also about his disappearance?"

"His name is Robert Oakley and he was one of General Waller's soldiers who remained here to help Colonel Massey. Bob's a sergeant and he was billeted in Eastgate Street. Three evenings ago we met briefly and he promised we would walk again by the river. Since then he has vanished."

"Vanished?"

"His kit has gone and no one seems to have seen or heard from him."

"Strange," Faith said, "but do not worry, Peg. Soldiers have special, sometimes secret, duties. There are however lists and I know who has access to them. Do not fret any more. Leave me to find out about your Sergeant Oakley."

"Oh thank you, Miss!" Peggy flung her arms round Faith.

The case of Sergeant Oakley nagged at the back of Faith's mind along with other matters. Preparing yesterday's meal for the committee and the visiting lawyers, meant she had to return plate and cutlery to her mother's household. She would do so then ask Richard Gwinnett afterwards about Peggy's missing Sergeant Oakley.

"I am making bed frames for St Bartholomew's hospital," Nathan said at breakfast. "Colonel Massey has ordered the worse wounded to be taken there, as the sights upset some of the housewives billeting them. They are not so capable as you are."

"I try to be capable," said Faith, "though the same sights upset me. I hope that those poor men at St Bartholomew's are not out of mind for being out of sight. We must still help them."

After the meal had been cleared away, Faith and Peggy set off for the Pury household leaving Mrs Curtis with the twins. On the way, Faith told Peggy she had not forgotten about Oakley.

"I must talk to my mother," she explained, "and settle the disruptions of yesterday. After that I shall see about your friend. There is sure to be a perfectly reasonable explanation."

To Faith's surprise, her mother was in a jolly mood.

"I'm glad you've come," Hortense said, patting her bed for Faith to sit on it. "I want to hear everything."

"I do not understand, mother."

"Come, come my dear. Remember I was once a women of the world." Mrs Pury gave a blissful smile.

"Yes mother."

"So you can't fool me about Richard Gwinnett."

"I don't understand."

"Don't you, my dear? Let's be honest," Hortense took Faith's hand, "at least among ourselves. You're my daughter. My flesh and blood. Like me, you're a human being first and a Puritan second. I saw you yesterday flirting with him. He's handsome I warrant you, not like that cadaverous husband of yours."

"Mother! Nothing of the kind took place and, anyway, you were up here in bed."

No, my dear. There was such a fuss going on, I decided to have a look. I saw you and Richard Gwinnett in the dining room. The way you glanced at each other . . ." Hortense Pury smiled. "Your secret is safe with me Faith, provided you tell me all."

"There's nothing to tell."

"All!"

"I repeat, there's nothing to tell. I did nurse Richard twice and he is naturally grateful. He would do nothing dishonourable, yet he makes me laugh."

"You certainly were laughing in the dining room. It did my heart good, only I couldn't see what you two were actually doing at the time. Come on, Faith. You must tell me. Did he kiss you?"

"No."

"Did he try?"

"We never touched."

"Then what did happen in there? It sounded strange."

"It was strange, mother, and I do not quite know how to explain it." Faith lowered her voice. "I asked Richard if his right arm still hurt and do you know what he answered? He said not so much now the feeling was coming back into his hand. Richard told me he had heard of this from other wounded soldiers and it was true. He could now move every missing finger."

"That is peculiar." Hortense Pury was wide-eyed.

"Then he said, 'I can touch that table. Indeed, if you held my right hand Faith, I could feel it."

"And did you?"

"No, at least not at first. But he insisted and, in the end, I touched what was not there. 'Now,' Richard said, 'I can feel your hand in mine. Can you feel mine?' Do you know mother, I believe I did. I cannot explain it, but his missing right hand was there, clasped round mine."

"Well, well." Mrs Pury gave a crooked smile. "It is fortunate your secret is between us. I could imagine some of our Puritan preachers making a grand sensation of what you have told me."

"Mother, you made a promise."

"And I'll keep it, my dear. I already keep a great deal hidden. Memories. Follies. Matters that Puritans call sins. But what of Richard Gwinnett? Do you intend seeing him again?"

"We may meet." Faith decided it was time to end the conversation. Was she not on her way to see the same man about Peggy's missing sergeant?

Faith Merrett felt twinges of guilt on leaving her parents' house. Suddenly she was full of doubts and fears. As if to reinforce these, the sky had become dark. Heavy clouds and distant thunder proclaimed an approaching storm. Added to such portents were the sounds of enemy cannon.

"Are you all right?" Peggy asked when her mistress hesitated in the street.

"Of course," Faith replied. "You'd better get back to Westgate, while I go and see about Sergeant Oakley."

"Thank you," said Peggy, before hurrying along the road.

Still Faith remained in the street. Helping Peggy, would mean seeing Richard again. In her heart she realised it was not necessary to ask Lieutenant Gwinnett. John Dorney, or even her father, would do as well. Yet also in her heart, Faith wanted to see Richard. It was a new feeling and it had come to her for the first time in her life.

"Lord guide me," Faith prayed silently before making for the Town Hall.

Later some soldiers came hurrying along the street.

"Hold on!" one cried.

"Keep moving," their corporal called over his shoulder.

"But there's a woman lying here."

The squad paused and looked at Faith. Her bonnet had rolled to one side, her fair hair was soaked in blood and she was quite dead. The cannonball that had killed her lay nearby.

An hour later, Faith's body lay in Nathan's workshop. Her husband hollow-eyed and white-faced, together with Thomas who was weeping openly, were fashioning her coffin. In the house, everyone mourned. Only the twins continued to smile.

When Colonel Massey heard the news, he too went to console the Purys. In addition to wondering what effect this death would have on the alderman's resolve, Massey had other worries. The Royalists were pouring fireballs into the city. On his way to the Merretts, he had witnessed a hit on the house of Mr. Comelines the apothecary followed by people desperately fighting the flames. And the dreadful day had not yet ended.

When Captain Alan Pury reported for duty later that day, Pudsey ordered him back home.

"My father told me to come," said Pury.

"What's this?" asked Colonel Massey emerging from his room. "Are you disobeying orders?"

"No, sir, but it is too sad at home."

"Well, you shall not go on the walls tonight. There happens to be a project more suited to your feelings and the needs of Gloucester. Our friends in the surrounding countryside will want to know if we are still holding out. So your duty is to make and light four torches at the top of the cathedral."

"Yes sir," Alan Pury brightened.

"I shall come to see the results," said Massey, "an hour after sunset. One final order, Captain and you will obey it. Once the torches are well lit, go home and comfort your father."

After young Pury had left, Pudsey asked Massey,

"Were you going to have torches tonight?"

"No, but I had to think of something."

As he went to carry out Colonel Massey's instruction, Pury was still stupified by the tragic event of the day. However, once inside the cathedral, thoughts of Gloucester, civil war and the tragedy to his family began to fade. The young captain could almost feel the weight of ancient stones, hear monks chanting from past centuries. He was not a religious man by nature, but the suddeness of Faith's death had unbalanced him.

"Steady sir," said his sergeant. The empty, cavernous cathedral was dark and full of rubbish. They began the long climb to the top of the tower.

An hour after sunset, Colonel Massey set off for The Cross accompanied by Pudsey. Enemy shot was still falling on the city, bringing tiles and masonry down into the streets.

"Do have a care, Edward," Pudsey kept saying. "We don't want to lose Alderman Pury's daughter and our military governor in one day."

"Highly unlikely, Henry."

"Where are you making for?"

"St John's. Fine view of the cathedral tower from there."

Between St John's Church and Northgate, there was an open space used as a market area in times of peace. A crowd of soldiers and citizens had gathered in the square. Following their gaze, Massey and Pudsey looked up at four torches blazing on the cathedral tower. Then Captain Gray came forward and saluted.

"Good evening, sir."

"Evening. What do you think of the torches?"

"Fine sir, apart from the enemy guns trying to hit them."

"I suggest you clear the square . . ." Pudsey began. At that moment, the stonework next to him exploded into fine dust. The next instant, Massey felt a bullet pass by his head and cried,

"The devil! Someone is shooting at us."

By then, all was confusion in the square. People began shouting and running in every direction. Only Massey stood still — until Pudsey and Gray pulled him into a doorway.

"Surely," Pudsey protested, "you don't want the Royalists outside to get you?"

"You mean Royalists inside," Massey said. "Those shots came from within St John's Church."

Calling soldiers to him, Captain Gray rushed into the dark building. There was more shouting and scuffling before two men were dragged outside. One, who Massey recognised as a farrier, was small and wiry, while the other — a big broad man — he had not seen before.

"Why were you two firing at me?" Colonel Massey demanded.

Neither man replied.

"Come Edward." Pudsey seized his commander's arm. "This may be a bigger plot than you realise. I am taking you away from here. Captain Gray, escort your prisoners to a magistrate, find out what happened and report to me at Greyfriars."

As night deepened, the King's wrath continued to fall on Gloucester. Fires were started and smoke lay about the city. In the Merrett house, Nathan maintained a vigil beside Faith's open coffin. His Bible lay before him and his fingers kept turning the pages as if endeavouring to find an answer there for his wife's death.

Several other people had prayed beside the coffin — the Purys, Mrs Curtis, Peggy, Thomas and the neighbours, but one by one they left. Tom was the last to leave, his heart aching as if it would burst. Since the deaths of his parents at Down Hatherley, Faith had become the person he loved best in a hostile world.

Tom went outside and unseeingly watched fireballs falling on the city. He reflected that these missiles and the enemy sending them should be regarded with anger, yet he only felt numb abhorrence. The whole situation was mad. Formerly war had excited him. Now it had come and he had seen what it entailed, Tom wanted no part of it.

During a lull in the firing, he noticed people hurrying towards The Cross. Many carried lanterns and there was an air of excitement which made Tom join them. At least it helped to obliterate the thought of Faith lying dead in her coffin.

Off Southgate Street there was an open space round a permanent platform on which stood the town pillory and gallows. From the lurid lights of lanterns and torches set at the corners of the platform, Tom could see a figure jerking on the gibbet. Nearby were Under Sheriff Hill and his assistants with another prisoner. Tom turned away in disgust. There seemed to be death everywhere.

A dull thud was followed by an agonised scream. Another thud sounded and there was more screaming. The crowd around Tom growled their approval.

"Serve them right," a man said to Tom as two more thuds and shrieks reached the boy's ears. "Trying to kill Governor Massey."

"Who are they?" As Tom asked, the crowd pressed forward. The man who had spoken to him went with the rest, but an old hag said,

"They hung one of them farriers. I knew him well. A nasty bit of work."

"Who's the other? What have they done to him?"

"Oh, he was the city's mace bearer. You must have seen him looking so important in them processions. That was before the maces were sold to pay for the war."

"What have they done to him?" Tom repeated.

"Chopped off his fingers and thumbs. He won't be carrying no more maces," the hag cackled.

As he ran back to Westgate Street, Tom kept flexing his own fingers.

The intense Royalist bombardment of Gloucester died away during the early hours of Saturday 26th August. The King's gunners had thrown everything they could at the city. In addition to iron and fire balls, they had used lengths of heavy chain, stones and six foot logs. These various projectiles did a great deal of damage to property and wounded several, though only one person was killed. Faith Merrett had been the sole victim of those terrible twenty-four hours.

Her funeral was due to begin at ten and, half an hour before that, the coffin emerged from Nathan Merrett's house. It was carried by the six soldiers billeted there and to whom Faith had been kind.The men had insisted on this task.

Immediately behind them came Nathan, white faced and unseeing, with Thomas beside him. They were followed by Alderman Pury leaning heavily on a stick, Mrs Pury the 'invalid' walking quite upright, Faith's favourite brother Alan and the rest of the family.

Colonel Massey was present, also John Dorney, Dennis Wise, Tobias Jordan and the rest of the committee. After them came scores of people for Faith was well loved in Gloucester. Among the mourners walked Richard Gwinnett, his face a mask of grief, and Peggy the maid sobbing continuously.

Seeing his church so full and having such a suitable subject on which to disclaim, the Puritan preacher rose to impassioned heights of eloquence. The younger, the better, the more untouched by the world a person was, the preacher maintained, the sooner God wanted to claim that man or, in this rare case, a woman.

"For I am a jealous God," thundered the Puritan.

Afterwards they went to the burial ground. Massey feared that Faith's father might fall into the open grave, for Pury stood swaying dangerously near its edge. The colonel was relieved when Alan Pury stepped forward and supported the old man.

As everyone dispersed, two new relationships were formed that were to have further consequences. The first was between Tobias Jordan and Nathan Merrett.

"Let me walk back with you," Tobias said.

Nathan nodded dully.

"We are fellow Puritans," Jordan went on, "sustained both by our religious beliefs and the help we must offer each other. You need help Nathan and I am going to give it to you. Apart from your present distress, you have family commitments, a household to maintain and — if I may say so — not much money because of this war."

"All you say is correct."

"I have been watching you, Nathan. I have heard you are as weary of this country as I am. That you have spoken of going to the New World when this worthless war is over. I have similar plans, also valuable contacts in Bristol. How much better to pool our resources and to help one another in the true Puritan spirit."

"You are too kind, Mr. Jordan." the light began to return to Nathan's eyes.

"Tobias please. Like yours, it is a good Biblical name."

"Tobias, you have given me hope."

"I am going to give you much more, Nathan. I have instructed my daughter, Prudence, to act as your housekeeper as from today. She is a dutiful girl is Prudence. She obeys me and she will obey you. In everything, Nathan. You will, I know, come to treasure her."

For one desperate moment, Nathan Merrett attempted to evaluate this further arrangement, but his mind was still numb. He remained silent.

The second development was between Richard Gwinnett and Peggy the maid. As Richard was making his way back to the Town Hall, Peggy approached him.

"Lieutenant," she said, "could you spare me a moment?"

"I am more a civilian now," he replied, "and not too fully occupied at that. What is the matter? You seem doubly distressed."

"I am, sir!" Peggy cried, then she blurted out her worries about Sergeant Oakley. "I've asked and I've asked, but no one can tell me anything. Mrs Merrett was going to see you when . . ." At the thought, the little servant girl began weeping again.

"Please," Gwinnett tried to comfort her. "Mrs Merrett would not wish you to act in this way. As for your missing friend, I would be happy to try and find him for you. There is, I am sure, a perfectly reasonable explanation."

Back in the office, he put the problem to John Dorney.

"It should be a simple matter," the town clerk said. "We hold all muster rolls, billeting lists and food issuing records. Sergeant Oakley did you say?"

Five minutes later, Dorney looked up from the sheafs of paper and remarked,

"There's something strange here. Two sergeants, not one, seem to be absent, yet remain on the strength. Sergeants Oakley and Summers. Ex-Waller men. We also appear to be short of four horses."

"Desertions do you think?"

"No," John Dorney said slowly. "Their captains have signed and Sergeant Major Pudsey initialled the muster rolls, but food has not been issued to them. I should have noticed this before. Leave it to me, Richard. I'll go and see Pudsey. There may be some military reason."

While this conversation was taking place, Colonel Massey pondered on another problem in the south east sector of the city wall. During the night, enemy sappers had dug a deep trench to the drained moat, protectng themselves with thick planks and sods of earth. Now, while gunners and musketeers gave covering fire, the same sappers were filling the moat using faggots and more earth. It was the classic prelude to a storming attack.

"Damned Forest miners," remarked a soldier in the Town Regiment. "Gloucester'll never forgive them."

"I'm glad you've come, Henry," Massey said when Pudsey arrived on the scene. "We have trouble here."

"And we have trouble back there," the sergeant major nodded towards the town hall.

After they had discussed the two situations, Massey said,

"I shall go and see Pury. Meanwhile you take over here. It looks like a sortie."

"We'll lose men." Pudsey was doubtful. "The enemy are in considerable strength."

"Wait until night, then use two hundred men, followed by another hundred. That trench system must be cleared and the covers torn open. I am off to see the Alderman. Do not worry about it, Henry. Sending the two messengers was my responsibility."

"Which I aided and abetted," Pudsey said.

Colonel Massey noted that neither John Dorney nor Richard Gwinnett glanced at him as he entered the outer office. In the inner office, Alderman Pury sat shrunken behind his desk. The muster rolls lay before him.

"Colonel," he spoke in a weary voice, "I am sure there is an explanation for this."

"There is, sir."

"Perhaps you would sit down and explain. But make it brief. I am not at my best today."

In three short sentences, Massey told Pury what he had done. A long silence followed before the alderman remarked,

"I am disappointed in you, colonel. For two reasons. We did agree to keep each other informed on all important matters. Also, contacting Parliament is my political responsibility."

"The messengers were on military business. To Sir William Waller. His own men."

"Come now, colonel. You are splitting hairs. I am not a simpleton and it is not worthy of you."

"I acted as I did," said Massey, "so as not to arouse alarm and despondency. The situation is becoming grave. I considered that secrecy was important."

"Unfortunately the matter is now in the open. I cannot conceal it. The committee of defence has to know. I should therefore appreciate you and Sergeant Major Pudsey being here in an hour's time."

"Talk, talk, talk," Massey said bitterly, "while the enemy presses us all the more."

"And I am being pressed by a growing Peace Party, sir."

"What party?"

"I am referring to some of the city's leading Puritans headed by Councillor Jordan, whom you also by-passed when you secretly sent those messengers. I shall do my best for you colonel, because I need your help. However we could all do with better news soon on the military side."

"Then give me three hours instead of one, sir."

Against his better judgement, Colonel Massey ordered an immediate sortie. He led it himself. The enemy fire was intense and, though Massey did not suffer a single scratch, many of his soldiers fell around him. At least they were able to tear up trench boards and throw grenades into the workings, leaving the system a mess of mud and blood.

"We have achieved little," Massey told Pudsey on his return.

"At the expense of some good men."

"I know, I know!" the colonel shouted. "Let me go and change for this cursed committee. I am relying on your support, Henry, for I am weary with fighting."

The meeting was a full one with Massey first giving an account of the latest sortie.

"We shall try again," he concluded, "after nightfall."

"May God go with you," Alderman Pury murmured. "But we must discuss the matter of you secretly sending two more messengers to London."

"At least they were not sent to Parliament," Pury went on, "which is our prerogative, but to your old friend Sir William Waller."

There followed a long silence, apart from Tobias Jordan whispering to Nicholas Webb and Robert Tyther on either side of him. Both were rich traders and staunch Puritans, representing a large body of opinion in the city. Eventually Jordan spoke in his lawyer's voice — penetrating and highly doubting.

"While I should like to accept the military governor's explanation and apology, I would also wish for more facts. For example, I am supposed to act as liaison between himself and this committee, so why did he keep the matter from me?"

"I believed it right at the time," said Massey, "and I still do. Secrecy is an essential of war. The military situation has worsened in the last few days. Speaking for myself, I am heartened that those two most capable sergeants are on their way to London."

"Are we not assuming a great deal?" Jordan addressed the meeting. "We have only a professional soldier's word that the two sergeants are on their way to London. Could they not now be with other er, professional soldiers outside our walls? Might they not be discussing plans on how to take Gloucester?"

"Sir!" Edward Massey leapt to his feet, his sword half drawn. "That is a slanderous lie and I'll . . ."

"Sit down!" said Pudsey, clamping one hand on Massey's shoulder and the other on the sword hilt. As the colonel reluctantly sat, the sergeant major rose, his large frame dominating the council table.

"Gentlemen," he said, "I must first nail the lie that Colonel Massey is communicating with the enemy. Throughout this siege and for many months previously, he has done everything possible in your best interests. Less than an hour ago, he was outside the wall risking his life for you. No one in this room, including myself, is worthy of criticising his loyalty.

"As to the incident of the two sergeants, I was there. I briefed the sergeants on Colonel Massey's instructions. They were to travel and see Major General Sir William Waller. No one else. He would listen to them, understand the situation and speak to the Earl of Essex. At the very least, our messengers would strengthen the pleas of those you sent."

"Or, on the other hand," Jordan interrupted, "you could both be in the same plot. Did you not also keep the matter secret? Did you not maintain your deception daily by faking the muster rolls? Only when you are found out, does this story about Waller come to our ears. And who is Waller? He was a failure who likewise abandoned our cause."

"Sergeant major," said Pury, "would you please reseat yourself. Tobias, I am having difficulty in following your reasoning. Assuming that Colonel Massey and Major Pudsey have secretly conspired to contact the enemy for a cessation of hostilities, would that not accord with your own views?"

"I do not understand you, sir."

"I am referring to the formation of your so-called Peace Party. It is my understanding that persons of your persuasion want to end the siege on the best terms obtainable, then leave Gloucester and England for the New World. If that is the case, would not the alleged efforts of Colonel Massey and Major Pudsey match your own aims?"

Again Jordan conferred with Webb and Tyther. When he voiced their collective opinion, it was less strong but still highly doubtful,

"We have never by-passed the committee and therefore we are still concerned with the case that has come to light."

Pury turned to Massey,

"Before I put the matter to the vote, colonel, do you have any more to say?"

The military governor shook his head.

"And you, sergeant major?"

"Yes," said Pudsey. "We are but soldiers. Our lives are fitted to wars and killings. Dirty work, gentlemen. Like the work you give to your under sheriff. However, lives such as ours, lead us towards reality. The reality of situations. We must assess them then act.

"Again and again during this siege, I have seen Colonel Massey presented with seemingly impossible situations. Yet, every time, he has come up with an answer. He listens, thinks and acts more swiftly than the rest of us. That is why gentlemen, I did not query him sending out the two sergeants. That is why gentlemen, I aided and abetted him.

"Let us not fool ourselves. Should we attempt to give in to the King, either by secret action or by some peace party, none of us will live to tell the tale. It is too late. We have gone too far. The siege is like wading across a river. Perhaps we are still going downwards. Perhaps we have reached the lowest level. Whichever is the case, we must keep on in order to rise to the other bank. So do not try to deflect the man in front — feeling the way, leading us across."

"You've convinced me, sergeant major," Pury remarked and most of the council members nodded. "What do you say, Tobias?"

But before Jordan could answer, Pudsey turned on him,

"As for you, do not fool yourself that the Royalists will let you sell your property and depart to America. Those days have passed and will only come again if we win. Should we be defeated, the King will exact his revenge for all the trouble Gloucester has caused him. Your precious businesses and properties will be taken from you and those of your persuasion. Your wives and children will be turned out to fend for themselves. Your bodies will be made to suffer until you look forward to the gallows. Forget your law, lawyer. Remember instead Prince Rupert of the Rhine. What happened when you met him."

"What did happen," Massey enquired as he and Pudsey were leaving the town hall, completely exonerated, "when Jordan met Prince Rupert?"

"He was," Pudsey replied, "rather scared."

Reports from the wall were bad. Notwithstanding recent raids by the Parliamentarians, the Roylists were rapidly repairing their trench system under heavy covering fire.

"Rupert's behind this," said one officer. "We've seen him here, there and everywhere. A cavalryman down in the bowels of the earth, I ask you. But he keeps at it and makes sure the others do the same. There are regular army sappers by the score and Forest miners by the hundred. I've also heard that more and more Welsh are being ferried across to join in the digging. They are like rats infesting the ground."

"Then we must be like terriers," said Massey. "More of our cannon will have to be brought here and depressed as far as possible with grape instead of shot."

"We are using more gunpowder than is being produced," one captain said but Massey ignored him.

"Then tonight," the colonel continued, "attack after attack. We shall bring in men from other quieter sectors. We must also use the citizens of Gloucester. They are smarting from the bombardments. We'll let them off the leash — like terriers as I said."

The sortie made by over a hundred Gloucester men was the most successful one that night. This party was led by Under Sheriff Hill and included most of his cronies. They relied on innate cunning, bulging muscles and sharp butcher knives. Their assault was so horrible, an entire section of seasoned Royalist troops broke and ran. Moreover, when Hill and his men returned, they were carrying several budge barrels of precious gunpowder.

The enemy retaliated by shelling the city throughout Sunday. Missiles of every kind showered on houses and churches. At the same time, the trenches were repaired, covered over and the filling in of the moat continued. It did not take a military genius to see the ramp being built towards the already broken wall.

Despite Puritan protests, Colonel Massey insisted on Sunday working and retaliatory raids. He used Hill and his men again. He used fire and explosives to destroy the enemy workings. He sent out diversionary parties to harry the Royalists in other sectors. These activities petered out as darkness fell.

When Monday dawned, there seemed to be no activity anywhere along the enemy lines. Colonel Massey relaxed a little and was having breakfast when a lieutenant came to see him.

"Captain Mallery at Eastgate would like you to come at once, sir."

"Right." Massey laid down his fork and picked up his sword.

On reaching the fortified gateway, Massey ran up the steps to the battlements. From this elevation, he had a fine view of the enemy lines and trenches. Nothing appeared to be happening and Massey was about to enquire why his breakfast had been interrupted when Captain Mallery hastened towards him.

"Sorry sir, it's below. This way."

He led Massey through the guardhouse and down slimy stone steps to what had once been dungeons. There, in a dismal dripping cell, were half a dozen soldiers with their ears pressed against the damp wall.

"Listen sir," Captain Mallery said.

Colonel Massey listened and could plainly hear scraping and burrowing noises below where they were standing.

"What," Mallery asked, "do we do now?"

"We counter-mine," said Massey. "We want two dozen picks and shovels. Baskets to carry away the earth. And men who know how to dig. Fetch Under Sherif Hill. He knows where the muscle is in Gloucester."

George Hill had his own ideas. In addition to the picks, shovels and baskets, he brought along some twenty Forest of Dean miners, lately taken prisoner. He told them,

"Now's the chance to earn your keep."

Colonel Massey, who was no newcomer to mining and counter-mining, watched fascinated as the Forest men removed the stone flags of the dungeon, then dug themselves downwards. Soldiers and other helpers formed a line to remove basket after basket of wet sticky earth.

"Why have you stopped?" Hill shouted down the hole when no more baskets appeared.

"We've come to a spring," one of the miners replied.

Not believing him, Hill took a lantern, dropped into the tunnel and crawled forward. It was true. The diggings were rapidly filling. He did not see how the Forest men had worked up until then. Crawling back, Hill reported to Massey.

"The water's beaten us," he concluded.

"Has this gatehouse," the colonel turned to Mallery, "any other dungeons?"

"There's one on the other side."

"Good, We'll go there."

The second dungeon was used as a storeroom and first had to be emptied. There were holes in the walls for inserting torches, also the rusty remains of manacles. Under Sheriff Hill grinned.

"I could make use of this place. Come on," he suddenly shouted at the miner prisoners, who were still caked in wet mud from their last dig, "what are you waiting for?"

Again the flags were levered up and a tunnel started. Once more the Forest men dug relentlessly downwards, sending back a succession of fully filled baskets to be emptied outside. Over two hours passed before they reported another, stronger spring.

"It cannot be!" Hill stamped about in frustration. "Surely my forefathers did not build a gatehouse over springs of water?"

"They did," muttered a Forester who was knocked across the dungeon for his pains. Massey took Hill to one side.

"You've done as much as can be accomplished here. If we run into springs, so will the enemy tunnelling towards us. I would ask you to rest and feed your prisoners. They have worked hard. Captain, keep listeners down here and let me know what happens. I am going back to Greyfriars."

Back at headquarters, two reports awaited Massey — one good and the other bad.

The good news was that large masses of Royalist cavalry had been observed riding away from the area. All of Prince Maurice's men had gone and, it appeared, most of Rupert's.

"Splendid!" Massey pronounced. "It may mean there are Parliamentary forces in the vicinity. Perhaps councillor," he addressed Jordan, "my two sergeants were of some help."

"One hopes so," Tobias replied.

The bad news was the appearance in the enemy camp of several Roman-type siege engines. These were wheeled towers with protective planking and boarding bridges. Hurrying to see them, Massey estimated that each machine could hold sixty fighting men.

"Very well," he said to the officers who had presented him with the new problem, "now they've shown us their pretty engines, it is up to us to destroy them."

"You mean when they get closer?" one captain ventured to enquire.

"No sir."

"But they are deep within the Royalist encampment. Even out of cannon range."

"I have an idea about using our horse now their cavalry has left them. A little deception could take us right up to those towers."

Shortly after dusk, as night was deepening, Massey led a troop out of Northgate. They had not gone far when a Royalist sentry challenged him.

"Where are our lines?" Massey said wearily. "We've been in the saddle all day."

"To your right," the sentry replied. "Did you see any of them?"

"No," said Massey not slackening pace. His troop followed closely, including the horses bearing bundles of pitch soaked faggots.

The city troopers trotted past two more sentry posts before reaching the siege engines. Instantly the wood bundles were flung around the wheeled bases and set alight. As the flames spread, Colonel Massey rode boldly about the Royalist camp calling,

"This way! The siege engines are on fire."

His alarms increased the confusion. Enemy officers and men ran in the direction of the fires while Massey calmly led his troop back to the city. Minutes later he was standing on the battlements counting the conflagrations.

"Two, three . . . ah, four. The fifth tower does not seem to have caught fire, Henry."

"Four out of five, Edward is good enough."

"And not a single casualty." Massey could not help feeling pleased.

When Prudence Jordan arrived at the Merrett household, her first act was to find food and eat it. Her second was to look through Faith's wardrobe in which there were suprisingly few clothes though in good condition. Prudence planned to wear some and sell the rest, though for the moment she would move warily.

The Jordan girl had sufficient family cunning to let Mrs Curtis continue looking after the twins while Peggy did the hard work. They in turn were relieved at the lack of drastic changes. As for dealing with menfolk, Prudence adopted a different approach. Men were masters and, even a lad like Thomas Hobart, had to be treated with caution.

Prudence could assume an expression of intense interest combined with quiet acceptance. She exhibited these traits when Nathan Merrett was around. For his part, he was merely polite. In the case of Tom, who was after all Merrett's nephew and therefore family, Prudence tried hard to win him over.

"I know," she kept telling him, "I could never take Faith's place, yet someone had to help your poor uncle."

"Mm." Tom was non-committal.

"He says so little, I would appreciate your help, Tom. There's so much I have to learn. Those cows for example . . ."

"Mary and Martha."

"I know nothing about cows. I can't even milk one."

"Mrs Curtis or Peggy'll show you."

By coincidence, cows were the next problem to beset Gloucester. Up till then, the Welsh forces on the opposite bank of the Severn were content to remain where they were and keep quiet. They must have received orders for more positive action. Desultory firing broke out — mainly directed by the Welsh towards the cows of Gloucester.

The city retaliated by removing the cows, then firing back at the Welsh. Musket fire led to cannon fire. Night raids were made by both sides and one fight took place between boatmen in midstream. Meanwhile the cows could no longer graze on the water meadows. A system of hay rations was devised by John Dorney and preparations made for slaughtering cattle when supplies ran out.

Then another and more dangerous problem began to press on Colonel Massey. It was one he believed had gone away until it loomed larger than ever. The mining operations under Eastgate recommenced despite the spring water. Somehow, possibly by pumping, the Royalists had managed to overcome their problem and Massey was obliged to solve his.

"I would guess," he said to Pudsey and Mallery, "they are transferring surplus water to other deeper diggings. That would account for the mining work being interrupted. We need to know."

"But how, sir?" asked Mallery. "The mine entrance lies within their lines, guarded day and night by companies of dragoons and musketeers. We watch them and they watch us. Always on the alert they are.

"Could we not," Sergeant Major Pudsey suggested, "lift some roofing in between?"

"They maintain patrols." Mallery answered. "No sooner are we out of the gate then they're on us."

"Therefore," Massey said slowly, "we should not leave by the gate. Instead, we'll turn one of our dungeon tunnels upwards to emerge a few feet outside the city wall. Only a small hole is needed, large enough for three mud crawlers."

In the early hours of Friday 1st September, three men emerged from such a hole. Unseen in the darkness they crawled above the tunnel until an entrance could be effected. A long hour went by before one returned. He knocked on the gate and, when it was opened, fell inwards. His naked body was streaked with mud and blood.

"Your report," Massey asked after the man had been sponged, bandaged and wrapped in a blanket.

"We came upon four sappers, sir and had to fight desperately. I am the only survivor."

"Did you see their workings?"

"Yes sir, I did. They're extensive with pumps and sumps down side tunnels. The water's hampering them as it did us."

"What about the head of their mine? Did you manage to reach it?"

"Yes sir. It was eerie with six dead men behind me. I took one of the miner's lamps. They've begun a chamber under the gate, trying to support the roof with planks and timbers. Water everywhere. It will be difficult for them."

"A few more days then?"

"Yes sir." The man closed his eyes and groaned in pain.

"Thank you, soldier. You are excused duty until you are fit and well." The colonel turned to Captain Mallery. "I don't think we can play this trick again. Once those dead men are found, the Royalists will keep guards in and around their mine all the time. They appear determined to blow up the gate, then storm us through the gap."

Massey started to pace up and down. He hated problems he could not solve. This one had returned to baffle him. In the end he hit on a part solution.

"Captain."

"Sir."

"If we place cannon directly opposite the trenches and entrance to that mine, we cannot depress the guns low enough to hit them."

"Correct sir."

"So we place our cannon further along the walls — three on each side — and use the angle to obtain the distance. We then can drop heavy shot on the entrance and their troops surrounding it."

As soon as it was daybreak, gunners and citizens began moving six of the city's heaviest cannon to selected wall sites on either side of Eastgate. By noon, all was ready. Shot after shot fell on the mine entrance and troop encampments.

The Royalists were not long in firing back. Their heavy cannon struck at those on the city walls. Furthermore, the King's musketeers came forward in droves to direct intense fire against anyone on the battlements. The fight continued all day with soldiers falling regularly on both sides. Towards nightfall, the shot and shell reaching Gloucester became so strong the defenders were obliged to move behind the walls and cease firing altogether.

That night, listeners at Eastgate could hear work going on under them, yet were unable to retaliate because of enemy fire still pouring in their direction. Then Westgate reported attacks by the Welsh forces towards the long bridge over the river. The Royalists had an abundance of ammunition while the defenders were obliged to conserve theirs.

By Sunday 3rd September, Colonel Massey, the committee of defence and everyone else in Gloucester were becoming increasingly worried. Over the past three days, the situation had deteriorated.

"Another three such days," Massey had confided to Pudsey, "And we're finished."

Only the Puritans had the answer. Sunday was the Lord's Day and was not the Lord on their side? They would hold an even longer than normal church service. It was bound to bring success to their just cause.

Massey fretted as the service went on through the morning. Three and a half hours had elapsed when a messenger crept into the church and whispered to him.

"Sir, Sergeant Major Pudsey reports grave danger at Eastgate. He begs you to come at once."

Ignoring the preacher's outraged glare, Colonel Massey rose and left the church.

"What's happening?" he asked the messenger as they hurried across the city.

"Just about everything, sir. Royalist sappers have been taking barrels into the tunnel all morning. At the same time, their gunners are bringing supplies of cannon balls nearer to the city wall."

"So they can roll forward their guns," Massey nodded, "when the time comes."

"And their cavalry, sir, They're back in force. Massing opposite Eastgate."

All this and more Colonel Massey noted on reaching the gatehouse. It was the greatest concentration of enemy troops since the beginning of the siege. Company after company were being moved into position.

"Dare I ask, Edward," Henry Pudsey greeted him, "what we do now?"

"Send messengers to every church and halt those services. I want the committee members here. The congregations here. Every able-bodied citizen, men and women, here. Also get Hill, his assistants and his prisoners. Before Eastgate is blown, we must build earthworks behind it. Between these two points, tearing down houses for material. Then we must emplace cannon on top to hit the enemy when they try to storm us."

"All on the Sabbath," Sergeant Major Pudsey raised his eyes heavenwards.

Colonel Massey had to say this for the citizens of Gloucester — they came running. The city fathers were not long after them. Even the Puritan preachers grasped the situation and helped with their prayers. As soon as a goodly crowd had gathered, Massey explained,

"The enemy is about to destroy Eastgate by means of a mine deep below ground. In my experience, the gatehouse will not so much blow up as subside. The moment a breach appears, their foot soldiers will make for it. After that their cavalry will try to pour through the gap and scour Gloucester."

A low groan went up from the assembled company.

"Our only chance," Massey continued, "is to build a second line of defence behind Eastgate. Across where you are standing." He proceeded to give orders, separating the crowd into several parties. Then, when the work had started, Massey took Alderman Pury to one side and said, "It could go any way today. I would advise you to burn or hide what papers you think fit."

Due to the urgency of the situation and with so many people toiling, the embankment behind Eastgate grew visibly. By mid-afternoon it was a man's height and it continued to rise hour after hour. Presently cannon were hauled to the top and positioned behind sandbags reinforced by heavy timbers hammered into the soil. All the while, people kept glancing fearfully at the still intact gatehouse.

"It has gone strangely quiet outside," Captain Mallery reported to Massey. "Their troops of horse have again ridden away and there has not been a shot fired in the last half hour."

"Let me see." Massey climbed one of the side walls. "Such behaviour does not equate with blowing the mine." He gazed towards the enemy lines. Mallery was right. It no longer presented the menacing aspect of that Sunday morning. The only horsemen to be seen were a few officers. The rest, as Captain Mallery had reported, were gone.

Suddenly he saw a single Royalist leave the line and walk calmly towards the city.

"I don't believe it!" Mallery exclaimed. "He's carrying an old-fashioned bow."

While they watched incredulously, the archer fitted an arrow to the bow, aimed high and fired over the wall. The arrow landed in the new embankment, fortunately not hitting the swarm of workers. When it was retrieved, a piece of paper was found wrapped round the shaft and brought to Colonel Massey who read the following message,

"This is to let you know that Waller has forsaken you and Essex has been beaten like a dog. Yield to the King's mercy while there is still time otherwise when we enter there will be no mercy for such obstinate traitors."

"What do you think?" asked Alderman Pury when Massey brought the message to him. Pury was in his office with John Dorney. There were papers burning in the grate and piles more waiting on the desk. Near to hand lay a small portrait of Faith Pury as a child. "Colonel," Pury repeated, "what do you think?"

"Of the message?"

"And the situation."

"If they were going to spring that mine under Eastgate, it would have been done earlier today. Daylight is fading. Their troops are no longer at the ready."

"Perhaps," John Dorney said from beside the grate, "they'll attack tonight."

"No," Massey replied, "it is an operation best accomplished by day. When they can recognise each other. My view is that nothing will be done this Sunday and there are other signs to confirm this. As you will recall, their horse recently left us. Some returned this morning, but have gone again. I would guess they are nervous of another threat such as a Parliamentary relief force on the way."

"Ah!" Pury's tired old face momentarily lit up. "If it were so."

"There are further signs. The Welsh are leaving."

"Their main contribution to the siege," John Dorney remarked, "seems to have been shooting at our cows."

"We have been watching them from the cathedral. The Welsh are definitely retiring in small groups. Openly and officially it seems. All moving westwards. Marry that with that is happening on the east side of the city and a trend begins to emerge."

"Indeed." Pury nodded vigorously.

"There is more, sir. The Royalist forces from Worcester, who were covering Kingsholm, are decidedly thinner on the ground. Our captains opposing them believe that most of their men pulled out last night and more have been drifting away today. This message by arrow," Massey pointed to it, "is a last ditch effort to try our spirit."

"What now, colonel?" Alderman Pury enquired.

"If only we could rely on a signal from Wainlode Hill. We have had one false alarm. Who knows whether another would be true? A further trick. I'd like to be more certain."

"There is a way," Pury gave a wry smile. "A matter of sending out secret messengers. Last time colonel, you did not want us to know about the possibility of defeat. This time we are interested in news of success. I also have my plan ready and waiting."

The day was coming to a close when Richard Gwinnett, Thomas Hobart and two local farmers, who had spent the siege in Gloucester, were called to Alderman Pury's office. When John Dorney led them inside, they were confronted by Pury and Massey both sitting behind the desk. The Alderman began,

"We have an important mission for you. Listen carefully to Colonel Massey for it affects the future of Gloucester. Tonight, within the next few hours, success or failure of the siege will depend on your efforts."

"There is," Colonel Massey took over, "a good chance of success to our cause. You will know that the mine under Eastgate has not been fired. That many Royalist troops are departing. We have reason to believe their ring round the city is thin and becomes thinner. I suspect relief from London is on its way and the Royalists already know it. We wish to learn that ourselves and — if such is the case — the relief army must be told we are still holding out.

"My officers have reported to me that the weakest part of the ring lies around Kingsholm. The enemy forces from Worcester and the Midlands are in a hurry to get back over the Severn at Tewkesbury. There are still a few guards posted and a pretence of encirclement, but nothing to deter good riders on fast horses. Especially after dark. And I know you are all good riders, eh Tom?" Colonel Massey ruffled the lad's hair.

"You'll have to travel lightly. No weapons are required. All one needs Lieutenant Gwinnett is a left hand to hold the reins and you have that. You're my chosen officer for the mission and Tom here your guide, for he has been the same way before. He will take you to a farm below Cleeve Hill where Under Sheriff Hill's brother lives. It has a great barn, the largest in the area — in case you are separated.

"As for you two, my friends," Massey turned to the farmers, "once away from the city, I want you to make for Sandhurst, then Wainlode. You know we arranged for a beacon to be lit on the hill when relief was on its way. We believe those arrangements were tampered with by Royalists or their supporters. So you must ask questions of people you know as to the true situation."

"We're from Sandhurst, sir," one of the men said. "We'll soon find out."

"And it won't be from Mr. Bell either," the other remarked.

There were a few more details to be discussed before the four left. At the military stables, Richard Gwinnett selected a powerful though well-mannered horse. For his part, Tom took the pony that had served him well before. The local farmers looked greedily over the other horses. With luck they might be able to keep them.

Captain Alan Pury was on duty at the city defences opposite Kingsholm and gave them final directions.

"See the gap between those two campfires. Make for it. Last night there were six fires in that direction. The Royalists are certainly thinner on the ground. Even if they have patrols, which I doubt, you should get through. After that you are in the open. Their own horse went during the afternoon."

The local farmers offered to go first as they knew the ground. They picked their way forward and toward the gap between the two fires. Thomas, who came next with Richard following, thought it was too good to be true. Soon the fires were on either side, then fell away behind them.

"We're in luck," Lieutenant Gwinnett remarked five minutes later. "When shall we split up?"

"Any time, sir," the local man replied. "There's the outline of Wainlode against the stars, while Cleeve lies in that direction. You can't miss it."

Thomas and Richard travelled slowly through the night. Towards morning, clouds obscured the stars and a chilling drizzle began to fall. Tom was relieved when he saw the big barn. Leaving Richard by a copse, he went on and saw Under Sheriff Hill's giant brother feeding pigs.

"I know your face, lad," said Hill. You're from Gloucester, ain't you?"

Thomas told him what had happened, then Richard Gwinnett rode in from the copse.

"Yes, there's a Parliamentary relief force on the high Cotswolds," Hill informed them, "and the word is that Prince Rupert's around somewhere. Luckily, they're all far away from here. Come and have breakfast with us."

Mrs Hill, almost as huge as her husband, welcomed them. Several sturdy children played in the farm kitchen and contented gurgles came from a nearby monster-sized cradle.

"The family," Hill gave a proud wave of his huge hand. "All big uns, eh."

After a meal and tending to the horses, Tom received further directions.

"You climb Cleeve, then head to the right. Soon you'll come to flat uplands and there you should find them. But watch out for Rupert's troopers. You don't want to lose your other arm, do you lieutenant?"

Hill's directions proved accurate. After a long, lonely ride, Richard and Tom sighted the Parliamentary relief force moving slowly across the bare wolds and made for the nearest column. They were intercepted by outriders.

"You claim you're from Gloucester," said a cavalry captain. "Can you identify yourself? You sir, with the one arm, who are you?"

"Lieutenant Richard Gwinnett, sir. I fought with Ballard at Edgehill and later lost this arm in Sir William Waller's service."

"We can soon prove or disprove your story," the captain said. "There is a Sergeant Oakley with us who lately rode from Gloucester to London."

Oakley was called and quickly identified them. While Gwinnett was taken to see Robert Devereux, Earl of Essex, Sergeant Oakley asked Tom about Peggy and what had transpired since he left the city. He also told Tom his own story.

"Summers and I slipped out of Gloucester easily enough, but our troubles started near Oxford. We had decided to stick together and to pass well north of the city. Even so we were challenged and chased. While fleeing, a shot from a carbine brought down Summer's horse. I heard his leg cracking like a stick. We had been through much together and I wanted to stay, but he yelled,

"Go on, Bob! Go on to Waller."

"There were other adventures too long too relate now. At last I located Sir William only to find him a broken man. He told me the other messengers from Gloucester had already reached Parliament. A relief force was being formed under Old Robin, our Earl of Essex. In addition to battle seasoned troops and experienced artillery trains, new regiments were made up from London apprentices.

"I wanted to return to Gloucester, to my Peg, and was told the assembly point was a little village outside London called Heathrow. From there we headed westwards and, once again, passing Oxford caused trouble.

"The Royalists started harrying us but we were too strong for them. Then at Stow-on-the-Wold, Prince Rupert tried his usual mad charge and with the help of our guns, we gave him a bloody nose. We were in high spirits after that, until the weather turned wet and cold up here on the high Cotswolds."

Despite the miserable conditions Robert Oakley described, Tom was impressed by what he saw. The regiments of Parliamentary foot advancing in parallel columns were well equipped and in full strength. The artillery trains with their rows of waggons lurched between the lines of doggedly marching men. Swarms of horsemen guarded all sides. In front rode the Earl of Essex with his own regiment and colours flying.

"We're going to win," Lieutenant Gwinnett declared when he rejoined Tom and Sergeant Oakley.

In Gloucester, the morning dawned damp and cool for early September. As night faded, the watchers on the walls looked searchingly towards the Royalist lines. It was difficult to tell exactly what was happening. There were a few carts trundling past Llanthony and some boats heading downstream.

At their early morning conference, Captain Mallery told Massey that all mining activities outside Eastgate had been at a standstill for twenty-four hours.

"We sent out a patrol," Mallery went on. "It came within range of Royalist musketeers, but they held their fire. Since then, they too have departed."

"Encouraging," Massey said.

His other captains made similar reports. On the western sector, the Welsh had all but disappeared from across the Severn. It was the same to the north towards Tewkesbury and Worcester. However, the King's own troops of foot, horse and artillery were still present, comprising over 6000 men.

"So we must not be rash," Massey reminded everyone.

His warning was confirmed later that morning. The defenders sent out parties and, whenever one ventured near the King's troops, they were fired upon. Musket shots were invariably followed by cannon and once again Gloucester was bombarded. When the firing slackened, Colonel Massey ordered work to continue on the enbankment which had risen behind Eastgate.

"Who knows," he said to Pudsey. "The relief force may have been beaten and the rest of the King's army return to take us."

Despite his cautious attitude, Edward Massey was more confident than he had been for weeks. He said so to Pury that evening if only to cheer up the old man. The alderman seemed to be ill, mentioning a bad night which had left one side of his face drooping and a useless arm.

"You should be in bed, sir." Massey was concerned.

"Perhaps when we have seen this through." Alderman Pury tried to smile. "Alan tells me there was talk of a bonfire on Wainlode Hill last night, though it was difficult to see because of the rain."

When the committee of defence met, many members were convinced that the siege had ended and wanted the church bells rung. In the end, it was decided to wait and make sure. As Pury put it,

"The King is still outside our city."

Another day and night passed. Despite the worsening weather, doubts and fears in Gloucester were being replaced by rising expectations. Soldiers and citizens alike watched and hoped. The Puritans prayed. Pury felt slightly better. There was a strange silence everywhere.

When Thursday 5th September 1643 dawned cold and wet, the signs of Royalist withdrawal were at last unmistakeable. Every tent had disappeared, the pavilion taken down, the trenches abandoned. Through the steadily pouring rain, Colonel Massey watched dejected companies moving away after the waggons and carriages. Finally, all that lay around Gloucester was a ring of mud.

"Shall we send out scouts?" Pudsey asked.

"Not yet," Massey answered. "Let us not lose anyone today."

On the Gloucester side, 40 soldiers and civilians had been killed and 400 wounded. It was estimated that over 1000 Royalists had died to no avail.

During the day, people kept arriving from the country to visit relatives and friends in the city. They told of Royalists retreating everywhere. The King had left Matson House in a carriage containing Prince Charles. When last seen, the carriage horses were slipping and sliding on the muddy hill road to Painswick. Soldiers wrestled with the wheels but the King did not glance outside. The carriage curtains were kept tightly drawn.

After midday, excitement mounted in Gloucester. Outriders from the relief force loomed out of the rain. At this stage, no one noticed the terrible weather. Citizens and garrison lined the walls while the bells of Gloucester rang frenziedly above them. Continuous cheering greeted the Earl of Essex and the relief force he brought with him.

That night, Essex dined at Alderman Pury's house. The Earl noticed how crookedly Pury was sitting, compared to plump and radiant Mrs Pury in her best gown.

"I do hope your arrival," Hortense chatted away, "will stop my husband worrying. He worries so! I kept telling him, 'What's the use of being in charge if you can't give the worries to your subordinates?' "

Old Robin merely smiled.

"Now that it is over," Mrs Pury went on, "I think we should reopen our house in London and live a little."

"Unfortunately, it is far from over, madam," the Earl informed her. "We have not beaten King Charles in battle, merely raised a siege. As soon as my men are rested, I must march them back again. The majority of the relief force consists of tradesmen and apprentices, whose wives and masters require them. I pray we do not lose too many on the return journey."

In the Merrett household, Nathan allowed everyone to eat and drink to their heart's content. The entire Jordan family was there, feasting like locusts. Mrs Curtis became a trifle the worse for drink and had to be carried to her room. Sergeant Oakley went off with the excited Peggy. Tom and Richard were tired but content.

"Well Nathan," Tobias Jordan pulled Merrett to one side, "we have won. Tonight we celebrate and tomorrow we can talk about our future. My contacts are anxious to further plans for the New World. You realise it will mean selling this property, your business and getting rid of the apprentices."

"Yes . . ." said Nathan.

"There is another matter. The expedition will be to strict Puritan principles. No single men and women of marriageable age are permitted. But then you and my Prudence can easily remedy that. She considers you a worthy match and so do I. Therefore that's no problem."

"Well . . ."

"Think also of the twins. What future is there for them in England? Even if Parliament wins, there'll be prolonged opposition from the nobility and their supporters. Believe me Nathan. I am a lawyer and I know. The New World will offer your little girls . . . I seem to have forgotten their names."

"Anne and Jane."

"Ah yes, Anne and Jane. The New World will offer them so much more. A fresh start. A society of our own Puritan making."

"Where do you intend we settle?" Nathan enquired.

"In New England, of course," the Puritan answered, "at a site called Salem."

While Tobias Jordan was weaving a web round Nathan Merrett, Tom and Richard were also discussing the future.

"I don't want to go on with my apprenticeship," said Thomas, "though I suppose there is no other way."

"There is now," Richard assured him. "John Dorney tells me that apprentices are being freed — in London and here — to help the cause."

"I am not sure I want to be a soldier." Tom thought of those men hacking each other to pieces and shuddered.

"There are other ways of helping," Richard said. "One is producing food. Soldiers wounded in the Parliamentary cause are being given grants of land to farm. John tells me I am eligible for such a grant and have only to pick a suitable place close to the city. I was thinking of your Down Hatherley farm, Thomas — if you'll join me?"

Outside the Merrett's house, Gloucester was settling down at last. Occasionally a party of soldiers, laughing men and women, would pass along Westgate. People shouted good night to each other. Lights went out in the houses. The rain continued to fall.

After dining with the Purys and their guest of honour, Colonel Edward Massey set off on a walk along the walls. Sentries were still stationed at key points though many, Massey noted, were none to steady on their feet. One he had to prop up in a corner, another had a woman on watch with him. The colonel chose to ignore these incidents. A good commander knew when to look the other way.

After his tour of inspection, Massey returned to Greyfriars. The place was deserted and he was tempted to retire and sleep off the recent meal. However the Earl of Essex had made a request to him earlier in the evening and Massey decided to meet it. When Henry Pudsey looked in later, the sergeant major found his commander writing by candlelight.

"Surely," said Pudsey, "you're not still working?"

"Just finishing," Massey answered. "Old Robin told me I would be staying as military governor and asked what I wanted from Parliament." He picked up a sheet and read, "Ten thousand pounds to cover arrears of pay due to the Gloucester garrison and to equip them for the coming winter. One thousand more foot soldiers and two extra troops of horse. One hundred pistols, sixty carbines and as much gunpowder as possible."

"The Earl has given us 40 barrels of powder and three cannon rather than haul them back to London."

"Everything is gratefully accepted, Henry."

"Do you think," Pudsey sat down across the table, "do you really think Parliament will grant all you've requested?"

"No," said Massey, "but then I have asked for twice as much as I need. In the end they'll give me less than a quarter. You know politicians. They twist and turn, get themselves into messes, then rely on despised soldiers like us to extricate them."

"That is a cynical view Edward," Pudsey said. "For my part, I believe society is changing for the better. During the period of change, there will be a new role for us soldiers. It is the reason why I have come to see you. Friends in the relief force have told me of opportunities if I go with them. Parliament is planning a new-style, highly trained model army. Professionals are needed."

"Although I shall be sorry to lose you, Henry," Massey said, "you have my blessing."

"I shall always be grateful to you, Edward." Pudsey rose. "For serving under you. You were never indecisive. During the siege, we presented you with the most appalling problems and you solved every one of them."

"Go and do likewise," Massey gave a tired smile.

After Pudsey had gone, the colonel went into his inner room. How many nights he had spent there sick with worry? No one ever knew, would ever know. To the citizens of Gloucester he would remain the military governor who met every contingency.

'Now I can relax,' Edward Massey put his sword to one side, 'for a short while — as the war is not over yet!'

AFTERWARDS

Afterwards, the Civil War dragged on for eight more years ending with the Royalist defeat at the Battle of Worcester in 1651. During those troublesome times, Edward Massey fought throughout the length and breadth of Gloucestershire. In 1646 he took his seat in Parliament as Member for Gloucester. In 1660 he welcomed King Charles II back to England at the Restoration and became Sir Edward Massey.

But the second King Charles was no fool. He never forgot his dismal childhood days at Matson House during the Siege of Gloucester. The Merry Monarch's face would grow sad when he recalled carving his name on the panelling to while away the time, also that slippery retreat up the hill to Painswick. When he asked his father where they were going, the first Charles replied they had nowhere to go. Failure at Gloucester was King Charles I's turning point leading to eventual defeat and execution.

Following the Restoration, Gloucester did not find favour for expansion and reconstruction. Eastgate was in such a bad state after the mining, it had to be pulled down. Similarly the other gates and whole sections of the walls were left to crumble. The only rebuilding permitted was that of the cathedral which the Puritans, before they set off to the New World, had actually attempted to demolish.

While remaining loyal to the Crown, the citizens of Gloucester retained their deep belief in the Law stemming from King and Parliament. Had not Gloucester a Parliament House long before Westminster? Thus it was no accident that one hundred years later a descendant of Richard Gwinnett left Down Hatherley for the New World, became Governor of Georgia and was among the first to sign the American Declaration of Independence.